# Journey to Restoration

Penny and Kendall Cochran

i

Dedicated to our children, MacKenzie and Katie Cochran, and our niece, Linnea Adams. We are so proud of the women you have become.

And in memory of my mama, Yvonne Banner, who did not make it to see this book in print. I know how proud of me you were. Thank you for always believing in me and for showing me what unconditional love looks like.

# Table of Contents

**Redeemed *(verb): to* free from captivity by payment or ransom**

Isaiah 43:1b-2, 4

*Do not fear, for I have redeemed you;*
*I have called you by your name;*
*you are Mine.*
*When you pass through the waters,*
*I will be with you;*
*and through the rivers,*
*they shall not overwhelm you;*
*when you walk through fire*
*you shall not be burned,*
*and the flame shall not consume you.*
*For I am the Lord your God... you are precious in My sight,*
*and honored, and I love you...* (NRSV)

# Preface

**Testimony (*noun*): a firsthand authentication of a fact; evidence; a public profession (MW)**

Revelation 12:11

*But they have conquered him [Satan] by the blood of the Lamb and by the word of their testimony, for they did not cling to life even in the face of death.* (NRSV)

Penny

Revelation 12:11 has echoed in my heart for quite some time. I felt a strong need to share our testimony with whomever God wanted to read it. In 1997 God led me to start keeping a journal. Through these journals, I was able to remember what had taken place and the miracles of God in our lives. Early on, God put on my heart that I was on a pilgrimage. It is a pilgrimage of faith, hope, and love, a journey to restoration. The scriptures used and the versions of the Bible used were part of our journey at that point in time of our

The Lord has also led me over and over to 1 Corinthians 1:25, 27, 30, which says, *"the foolishness of God is wiser than men, and the weakness of God is stronger than men...But God has chosen the foolish things of the world to put to shame the wise, and God has chosen the weak things of the world to put to shame the things which are mighty... you are in Christ Jesus, who became for us wisdom from God..."* (NKJV) I have often lived my life in trying to please others. I have felt weak and

3

uneducated; I have felt foolish and have wanted to look "good" to others. Thankfully, God has been with me. This book is a stretch for me, as I tend to want to stay hidden. But, because I am in Him, He gives me His wisdom, courage, and strength.

So, in saying that, I have tried to listen to His voice throughout the writing of this testimony. I have prayed over Kendall as he wrote his story. It has been painful at times to relive the dark times in our lives. So, if you disagree with what I have written in any part, that is okay. In my heart, I know my "right standing" comes from God alone. But, even now, I struggle with what others will think. I am still on a journey, so I may get it wrong. It is for each of us to, as Philippians 2:12-13 says, *"work out your own salvation with fear and trembling, for it is God who works in you both to will and to do His good pleasure."* (NKJV) In this book, we are bearing our souls and confessing our sins, which can be frightening. I hope that in doing so, we are a light of hope to others. In shining light on the dark places, we can conquer our enemy.

Kendall

Most of the stories I tell about Penny and me are light-hearted and full of humor. However, there is another part to our story, and it is tough to admit. Even now, as I am writing, the fear of what people might think terrifies me. Will they see me differently, treat me differently, avoid me? But then I remember why we are writing the book - to show people that no matter how far you might wander away from God if you focus your attention on Him and His word, there is nothing so dark and terrible that He can't restore you.

4

# Part One

**Revived (verb): to return to life; to flourish (MW)**

Psalm 119:25-28

*My soul clings to dust;*
*Revive me according to Your word.*
*I have declared my ways, and You answered me;*
*Teach me Your statutes.*
*Make me understand the way of your precepts;*
*So, shall I meditate on Your wonderful works.*
*My soul melts from heaviness;*
*Strengthen me according to Your word.* (NKJV)

# Chapter One

**Strength (*noun*): the quality or state of being strong; capacity for endurance (MW)**

Isaiah 40:29-31

*He gives power to the weak, and to those who have no might He increases strength. Even the youths shall faint and be weary, and the young men shall utterly fall, but those who wait on the Lord shall renew their strength; they shall mount up with wings like eagles, they shall run and not grow weary, they shall walk and not faint.* (NKJV)

Penny

My childhood started like that of many other children in the mountains of Upper East Tennessee during the 1970s. During the summers, I spent my days turning cartwheels, playing in the water sprinklers, rolling down hills, and getting browner by the minute playing in the sunshine. It was a time when I could walk up the street to a friend's house as a four-year-old by myself, and my mom did not worry. I watched the cows over the fence with my daddy, played in the creek, and caught fireflies under the trees with my cousins.

But then, at age seven, I realized things were changing with my body, and I did not know what to do. My first instinct was to hide the problems from my mom and grandmother. When I walked on my toes, I told them I was practicing being a ballerina. In reality, I could not put my feet down. I stopped turning cartwheels. When I ran races with my cousins, I stopped to rest on the steps at the back of the house. I did not care anymore if they won. In the duck races, I found I could not squat to walk like a duck. My Uncle Art was diagnosed with polio as a child. He took my mom aside soon after watching me struggle and expressed his concern. The next day I found myself at my pediatrician's office. He was bothered by my symptoms as well.

Watching the cows with my daddy

On my eighth birthday in 1976, I found myself in Memorial Hospital in Johnson City, TN. They did not know what was going on with me, so I lay in bed day after day for two weeks. By the end of the two weeks, I could not walk or lift my hand to my mouth to feed myself. While I had walked into the hospital on my own, my dad had to carry me out. After seeing several specialists, my pediatrician sent me to Bowman Gray Hospital in

Winston Salem, NC, where the doctors ordered more blood work, tests, and biopsies.

Three weeks after first entering the hospital, the neurologist diagnosed me with Juvenile Dermatomyositis, an inflammatory skin, muscle, and blood vessel disease which causes skin rash and progressive muscle weakness. It can also cause pain, fatigue, fever, and calcium deposits under the skin and around the muscle and joint. I would end up having all of these symptoms. They started me on high doses of prednisone and sent me home.

After my return home, I started physical therapy three times weekly. My therapist worked on getting me back on my feet by teaching me to use a walker. One of the side effects of prednisone is weight gain. I went from a girls size 8 to a girls size 16 quickly. Mama joked that when breakfast was over, I was already asking what we were having for dinner. I looked like a chipmunk as my face ballooned along with my body. My weight would fluctuate throughout my childhood depending on how much prednisone I was on at the time. My potassium level bottomed out, causing even more weakness. Along with eating innumerable bananas, I also had to drink foul-tasting potassium in liquid form.

With my sister, Cyndi before diagnosis, age 7

After diagnosis, age 8

I am not sure how my mother handled all that she had to do. I could not walk. I had to be dressed, carried, and bathed. My sister was still little more than a toddler. But Mama always had dinner on the table by five when my dad came home from work. I was supposed to do exercises at home as well. My mom and dad had a hard time getting me to walk with the walker or do the exercises at home. Finally, my dad made me mad enough by telling me that I *could not* do it that I forced myself up to prove him wrong. I was a strong-willed child – a trait that helped me over many hurdles. Although, I am sure my parents and sister did not always appreciate this part of my personality.

At age nine, I was having trouble even standing up due to extreme pain in my back. The high doses of prednisone had caused my bones to weaken, and I had developed spinal fractures. I had finally grown my hair out so, the thing I remember most about this hospitalization was having to have all my hair cut off because it was so matted from lying in bed. I missed my grandmother most of all. From my hospital bed, I talked with her on the phone. I loved her dearly and wished she could come to me, but she was not well. My grandmother died in April 1977, three months before my tenth birthday.

My dad had to work overtime hours to make more money to pay all the medical bills, while Mama had to be with me in the hospital. Since Dad had to work, my sister stayed with relatives. Cyndi was only three years old when I was diagnosed and must have felt abandoned at times. My parents and extended family spent many hours in prayer for me. Our church came together for a twenty-four-hour prayer vigil for me. God is faithful, and my parents' continued praise for His faithfulness gave my sister and me the building blocks for a strong faith.

In 1978, I discovered something else to hide from my mother. I found large bumps under my arms, which I assumed were cancerous tumors. I did not want my mom even more upset, so I decided not to tell her. One problem, however, was that I could not dress without my mother's help, so she soon discovered them on her own. Another

11

round of appointments ensued. Like the first time, no one in East Tennessee understood the problem, so my pediatrician referred me to a metabolic specialist at the Medical College of Georgia. The doctor admitted me for another two-week stay. This time, instead of leaving me in the bed, I walked the halls on a walker with physical therapy, played in the playroom, had occupational therapy to learn to get off the toilet by myself, and even attended school.

The hospital was a research hospital. It was also considered a welfare hospital, a term used in the 1970s, which provided free care to children in need. Most of the children on the pediatric wing were there because they were dealing with the effects of physical abuse or because their parents abandoned them at birth due to medical conditions their parents could not handle.

My roommate was a baby whose parents had deserted her because she had a heart defect, and while her external features were female, her internal characteristics were male. My mom stayed with me around the clock for two weeks and ended up being a calming influence for the baby. A little girl in a wagon who had lost her legs from being submerged in boiling water often came to visit me in my room. A little boy, who loved to play peek-a-boo with me outside my door, dealt with seizures due to a head injury from abuse. These children had a significant impact on me. One day I would seek God's purpose for my life, and these children would return to my mind.

During my stay at the research hospital, doctors used me as a guinea pig because my symptoms were rare. They studied everything about me. I had a vast number of medical students stream through my hospital room every day. During my first hospitalization at age eight, I had many scary tests completed. I shared with my mom the fear that I would have to have another EMG (Electromyography) or a biopsy of my muscles. The doctors had warned me they might need to repeat the tests. She told me that I needed to talk to God about it. I could ask Him not to allow the tests to happen. So, I did; I simply asked and believed he would take care of me. The next day the doctor said they had decided that there was no reason to repeat the tests. My faith grew exponentially that day.

Through all the years of health issues to follow, that line in the sand where I put my trust in Him was where God met me, and I crossed over with him. It helped me be fearless in the face of whatever life would throw at me because He was holding my hand. Finally, after two weeks, I was discharged with a research drug that they hoped would decompose the calcium around my muscles and joints. Unfortunately, it did not work; instead, it stunted my growth. During the next few years, the doctors tried numerous research drugs and withheld calcium in food and supplement forms in an attempt to get rid of the calcium deposits.

The muscle disease continued to go in and out of remission for the remainder of my childhood and teenage years. When I went out of remission, I would run a fever, become extremely weak, and then wake up to realize I had lost all the work I had put in during physical therapy. It was like having to go back to the starting line over and over. One of the treatments for the calcium deposits was ultrasound. Back in the 1970s, the ultrasound equipment was metal, so it was hard. Having the metal moved across the bumps was very painful, like rock moving over rock.

Even though I loved my physical therapist, this started to make me dread my therapy days.

From third through seventh grades, I received my education at home through homebound teachers. Thankfully, scarves were a fashion statement in the latter 1970s. I had ugly, bumpy calcium deposits on my neck, but the scarves hid them well. I desperately wanted to go to school. I missed having friends, but I would relapse each time I started back to school. Finally, beginning in eighth grade, I was able to start attending school on a full-time basis. I continued prednisone with weekly bloodwork and physical therapy but was able to lead an ordinary life. Thankfully, the deposits did at least stop growing and even receded from the surface of my neck.

Penny, age eleven, after baptism, pictured with Mama and Grandpa

When I could finally walk without the walker, my dad had found a new church closer to our home. He still had to carry me some, especially up and down the stairs, but I was at least getting to see people again. The prednisone decreased, but at this point, I had developed an adrenal gland suppression from the prednisone, causing me to lose weight. My appearance was disquieting for those who did not know me. I had become extremely thin, very pale, and had dark circles under my eyes. I also walked on my toes and could not straighten my arms. One day, a friend from church decided to put make-up on me. That day her dad commented on the increased color in my cheeks. One bonus was that my mom started letting me wear make-up earlier than all the other girls.

I made amazing, life-long friends at church and had godly youth leaders who pointed me in the right direction. My friends stood by me and helped when I was sick and treated me like any other teenager. We spent every moment together hanging out at each other's houses and with our youth group. We had sleepovers, talked on the phone, watched MTV, and ate massive amounts of junk food.

I still had periodic flare-ups of the disease, left early for weekly bloodwork, and missed quite a bit of school, but otherwise hid my illness well. I could not sit on the floor or even get up from the floor, so if there was not a seat, I just said I wanted to stand. I shared with one of my guy friends who knew about my condition that my greatest fear was falling and not being able to get up on my own. So, he walked me to class each day. Once, I tripped, but I did not even hit the floor because he caught me. I completed eighth through twelfth grade in public school and was able to walk across the stage to receive my diploma.

With help from my guidance counselor and the tenacity of my mom, I enrolled at East Tennessee State University (ETSU) with a full Vocational Rehabilitation scholarship. During the summer before starting ETSU, I had all the tests and biopsies from my childhood completed again. However, I was not afraid because I knew God was with me, and I realized that the pain would only be for a moment. With Him, I could easily handle a moment. The tests showed that the disease was still present. However, my doctor was concerned because I had been on prednisone for ten years, and he felt the effects of the prednisone would eventually be worse than the disease. So, he started me on methotrexate, a new treatment for rheumatoid arthritis. It worked wonderfully. I was ready for my new adventure as a college student.

# Chapter Two

**Faithful (adjective): given with strong assurance; true to the standard (MW)**

I Corinthians 10:13

*God is faithful, and He will not let you be tested beyond your strength, but with the testing He will also provide the way out...*(NRSV)

Penny

I chose ETSU for two reasons. First, I wanted to have a Bachelor of Social Work (BSW) degree. I needed to live at home to save money, and no other college in the Northeast Tennessee region had the Social Work program available. Secondly, I wanted to attend ETSU's Campus House. Campus House, or Christian Student Fellowship, is a college ministry at ETSU through the Christian Church.

I had gone to the house on one occasion for a retreat in high school and could picture myself there. A girl from my home church went to Campus House and encouraged me to come, but I was still nervous. I dragged as many people as I could with me. Even when they decided not to come back, I continued to go by myself. It was a small but fun group of students. Because I lived at home, unlike most students, it was a place to belong on campus.

During my sophomore year, I moved into the apartment on the second floor of the Campus House with three roommates. I loved living with my roommates and being at the house all the time. Our job was to lock up the house, and sometimes it was midnight before we could get everyone to leave. It is incredible how much a person can learn during the college years and not just academically. I thoroughly enjoyed every moment.

College years are always a time of revelation about oneself and how the world works and, hopefully, about how God works. My experience with dating in high school was limited at best, so it was a heady feeling to be noticed by guys for the first time. Once I lived away from home during my sophomore year, I began to date more. I had some one-time dates that never went anywhere. I had some guy friends who wanted to date, and I ruined the friendship by completely pulling away because I did not know how to handle it. I had guys I did not know come up and talk to me in restaurants.

My first experience with having a boyfriend in college was exhausting. It is hard to have school, work, and a social life. I went to class at ETSU from seven am until one pm every day. I clocked into my job at the mall at one-thirty and clocked out at closing. My new boyfriend worked in a restaurant. I would leave work and go and sit at the restaurant until he closed. Thankfully, I did get some homework done while I was there. He was three years older than me and had attended church as a child but had some negative feelings due to experiences with the church. So, we were pretty different. Even though I was crazy about him, I was still even crazier about God. So, I told God that if He did not want us to be together, please take him away because I did not think I could walk away. You always need to be careful when you pray that you mean it. God will take you at your word. We broke up.

I survived the break-up, although I am sure my friends were extremely sick of hearing about it. I did not just get through it; I grew. I cared about and respected this guy, so I gave him back to God. I had some specific prayer requests for him. First, I prayed that God would send him someone to connect with him and lead him back to God. Second, I prayed that he would move out of the house he was currently in, as some of his roommates had some nasty habits. Third, I prayed that he would go back to school, and finally, that God would send him someone to love who knew God. I drew another line in the sand. Looking back, it seems like quick work on God's part. I think it is pretty cool that God would care enough about me to let me know what He was doing.

One night, as I was sitting in the Wednesday night meeting at Campus House, a new guy asked us to pray for his new co-worker. They had connected at work, and he was talking to him about God. When he said it, I knew. But afterward, I went up and asked who he was talking about just to confirm. Yes, God answered my first prayer. Not long after, my mom was delivering cookies to recent visitors to our church. She could not find the house, so she went up to knock on a door to ask for directions. Guess who opened the door. He told her he had recently moved with a good friend. God answered my second prayer. I found out later that God answered the other two requests as well. Talking with his wife, years later, she told me that yes, she did know God when they started dating but that he had been pivotal in her growth with God. God was faithful to him and to me. He always has a perfect plan.

God is faithful. However, most of the time, we, humans, are not. After I had poured out my heart to God and He had demonstrated His faithfulness, I realized I was angry. God honored my first prayer of surrender: to take him away if it was not what God wanted. I had grown by praying for him and seeing God move. But I think in my mind, I thought once he started connecting with God,

God would give him back to me. I thought the "someone to love who knew God" part of my prayer would be me. Once I realized that was not God's plan, I was angry. Like a child, I rebelled. I found a new boyfriend, who professed to be a Christian. We even went to church together regularly. But his actions did not meet his words. I made some bad choices and followed him into some bad situations. Even in my sin, God protected me. I knew I was making some bad decisions, but I was not sure how to turn around. However, he made a mistake. He messed with one thing that was dear to my heart.

I had attended the Muscular Dystrophy Association (MDA) camp as a child due to my diagnosis. Once I was in college, I became a Unit Leader with the camp. I loved being with the kids. Because of their disabilities, each camper had a one-on-one counselor to take care of their needs. My boyfriend had interviewed to be a counselor and was supposed to go with me to camp. They were expecting him. He backed out the day before camp, leaving a camper without a counselor and the director scrambling to fill the need. You don't mess with my kids. I immediately broke up with the guy and then headed to camp. Most of the counselors at the MDA camp were not Christians. That year, however, God sent me one. He was a guy studying to be a minister. We spent every night talking about God. I confessed to him the things I had done and asked God's forgiveness. God's mercy and grace are precious gifts. It felt good to be with Him again.

Throughout my rebellion, I had also pulled away from Campus House. I lived at the Campus House during this time, and I know my friends were worried. I had scheduled myself to work on Wednesday nights, so I would not be at worship. I think I was afraid they would look me in the eyes and know what I had been doing. Thankfully, I returned to start my Junior year of college with a renewed heart for God. I found my friends waiting for me.

I Corinthians 1:7b-9

*... Jesus Christ, who will also confirm you to the end, that you may be blameless in the day of our Lord Jesus Christ. God is faithful, by whom you were called into the fellowship of His Son, Jesus Christ our Lord.* (NKJV)

Penny, age nineteen, at Campus House

# Chapter Three

## Hope (verb): the expectation of finding God[1]

Ephesians 1:17-19a

> the God of our Lord Jesus Christ, the Father of glory,
> may give to you the spirit of wisdom and revelation in
> the knowledge of Him, the eyes of your understanding
> being enlightened; that you may know what is the hope
> of His calling, what are the riches of the glory of His
> inheritance in the saints, and what is the exceeding
> greatness of His power toward us who believe...(NKJV)

Penny

I was baptized in 1978 at age eleven after confessing my belief in Jesus. I prayed and studied to the best of my ability at the time, but I wanted more. As a child, I loved the book, *Christy* by Catherine Marshall. It is a big book for a nine-year-old, but my grandmother shared her book with me, and I read it while I was sick in bed. Her book had a map in the front of it, and she said it was around the area where she grew up. The book disappeared when my grandmother died, so I was constantly looking for one with a map. It was ridiculously hard to find. While I was looking for an old copy of *Christy* in a used bookstore one day, I found another book by Catherine Marshall called *The Helper*. What caught my eye was not the title; it was

---

[1] Kyle Blevins. *"Why Faith, Hope, and Love Are So Important and Will Last Forever,"* Crosswalk (blog), 2021.

that Catherine Marshall had written it. The book was about the Holy Spirit and the help He could provide in my walk with Him. In my home church, I did not recall any teaching on the Holy Spirit. I knew He was part of the Trinity. I remembered memorizing the Fruits of the Spirit as a child. But, I did not truly understand who the Holy Spirit was.

So, after reading the book, I began to seek Him on my own. Many of the scriptures on the Holy Spirit seemed to say different things even within the books of Acts. My takeaway from my study was that I had received the Holy Spirit when I was baptized. John 3:5 says, *Jesus answered, "Most assuredly, I say to you, unless one is born of water and the Spirit, he cannot enter the kingdom of God."* (NKJV) However, I still did not feel I was getting everything He wanted to give me. I had always struggled with memorizing scripture and even in trying to study my Bible. I found John 14:26, which says, *"The Helper, the Holy Spirit, whom the Father will send in My name, He will teach you all things, and bring to your remembrance all things that I have told you."* (NKJV) And Acts 4:31, which says, *"And when they had prayed, the place where they were assembled was shaken; and they were all filled with the Holy Spirit, and they spoke the word of God with boldness."* (NKJV) I wanted boldness.

Alone in my room at Campus House in February 1988, I felt compelled to ask my Father for the gift of the Holy Spirit that I had read about in Luke 11:13, which says, *"...how much more will your heavenly Father give the Holy Spirit to those who ask Him."* (NKJV) The Spirit had always been there with me since I had given my heart to Jesus, but I think sometimes God wants us to ask for

24

more. As I sought the Father's heart, the Holy Spirit began to lead me through the scriptures and show me things He wanted me to learn. God gave me opportunities to talk to others about Him, even those on campus who did not know if they believed. I know God opened the doors for me to speak about my faith because some of the girls I talked with were vastly different from me. I joked that God must have written a sign on my forehead that said, "Talk to me. I will listen." I talked with girls who were suicidal, with girls who hated themselves and self-harmed, with those who drank too much or were putting themselves in bad situations with guys. I tried to answer their questions. When I did not know the answers, we studied and searched the Bible together. I was finally able to disciple other girls, lead Bible studies, and pray with others without fear.

In my studies, I read James 1:5, which says, *"If any of you lacks wisdom, let him ask of God, who gives to all liberally and without reproach, and it will be given to him."* (NKJV) I read through the gifts of the Spirit in 1 Corinthians 12 and decided that since God told us to ask, I would ask Him for the gift of wisdom. 1 Corinthians 12:7-8 says, *"But the manifestation of the Spirit is given to each one for the profit of all: for to one is given the word of wisdom through the Spirit..."* (NKJV) I knew I would need supernatural wisdom more than anything for my future career in social work and with the girls I was encountering on campus. I also needed to understand how to seek Him. God also taught me different ways to study scripture besides just reading it. Christian music was something that God used to help me learn. I loved Rich Mullins and his song, *Home,* called to me.

*And now the night is fading*
*And the storm is through*
*And everything You sent to shake me*
*From my dreams, they come to wake me*
*In the love I find in You* [2]

I started by looking in my Bible's concordance for the word shake, which led me to Hebrews 12. Hebrews 12:28-29 says, *"Therefore, since we are receiving a kingdom which cannot be shaken, let us have grace, by which we may serve God acceptably with reverence and godly fear. For our God is a consuming fire."* (NKJV) I knew that these verses were truth. Just as I wanted more from Him, He wanted more from me. He wanted my surrender. He wanted to be the consuming fire within me. I was close, but I was still fearful of what I might lose - not yet understanding all I would gain in the process.

During this time and in my journey with the Lord, I had concluded that healing was not possible. The calcium deposits in my body had remained stagnant since my early teens. In 1987 the calcium deposits began growing again. I began going back to my doctor at the Medical College of Georgia. He started me on some disgusting, chalky medicine which I had to take three times daily. He also told me to stop eating dairy. There were other children with dermatomyositis with calcinosis, but no solid research showed anything that worked. So, the medicines he put me on were all experimental.

During this time, I had a revelation. A new child came to MDA camp that summer. She also had dermatomyositis with calcinosis. However, she was

[2]Rich Mullins, "Home," track #5 on *Winds of Heaven, Stuff of Earth,* 1988, Reunion Records.

suffering- much more than I ever had. The calcium deposits were all over her and all at the top of her skin, many having broken open. She was medically fragile and extremely sick. She had infections continuously. I talked with her and her parents about my faith and prayer. Unfortunately, they were not Christians, they were hopeless, and they did not receive what I was saying. I also did some research on dermatomyositis and made some discoveries. When I received my diagnosis, some children did not respond to prednisone at all, and until the late 1980s, that was the only drug proven to work. Those children were just left weakened until they could no longer even swallow and then died. I realized how fortunate I was to be alive and that I knew my heavenly Father. He gave me a family who knew Him and taught me about Him and a church that believed in prayer.

I was discouraged, but I was not hopeless. I continued to seek God. Finally, the Lord led me to a scripture I had never noticed. James 5:14-15 says, *"Is anyone among you sick? Let him call for the elders of the church and let them pray over him, anointing him with oil in the name of the Lord. And the prayer of faith will save the sick, and the Lord will raise him up."* (NKJV) I did not feel led to the elders of my church but instead to my campus minister. I talked with him about the scripture. We had a group of students who were the core leaders who could stand in as elders. The second part of James 5:16 says, *"Confess your trespasses to one another, and pray for one another, that you may be healed."* (NKJV) One evening my campus minister and the student leaders met together. My campus minister talked with us about the scripture, and we took the time to confess our sins and pray for one another. They then prayed for me, anointed me with oil, and laid hands on me. To be truthful, I was a little disappointed; I do not know if I thought He would cleanse me of the calcium deposits instantly or if an angel of the Lord would appear to me in the night. Even though neither happened, I continued to have faith. By the Summer of 1988, my doctor felt I no longer needed medication for the muscle disease. I have never been on medication for or had a relapse of the dermatomyositis again.

However, even though the muscle disease went into permanent remission, the calcium deposits did not diminish. Instead, they began to pop open. I had drainage of calcium, a thin, toothpaste-like substance, seeping from several of them. I had to keep them bandaged and was put on a standing order of continuous antibiotics by my physician in Georgia. I had to change the bandage often because it would soak through. It was irritating and sometimes embarrassing, but it was not life-threatening. It kept me humble.

# Chapter Four

**Love *(noun)*: the clearest picture of God we have; love restores us to others** [3]

John 15:12-13

*This is my commandment, that you love one another as I have loved you. Greater love has no one than this than to lay down one's life for his friends.* (NKJV)

Penny

Campus House helped us to ask questions and seek God on our own. We had a huge amount of fun; however, we were also a growing group, seeking God together and separately. When we prayed together, a friend would always say to me, "Do you want to dial or hang up?" If one in our group was hurting, we were there for one another. Confession and accountability were encouraged and offered without judgment. We were not perfect, but we loved each other and attempted to be as inclusive as possible to share that love with others. I had just come off a summer of finding fresh grace. I wanted to show God how much I loved Him and wanted to serve Him and love others through Him. However, I had not yet fully realized the meaning of grace; grace is unmerited favor, a gift, not something to be earned. I just knew I owed Him so very much. I felt as if I was finally putting Him first.

Kendall

It was my second year at Milligan College, and I had finally put my priorities in order. I spent most of my time

---

[3] Kyle Blevins. "*Why Faith, Hope, and Love Are So Important and Will Last Forever,*" *Crosswalk (blog)*, 2021.

talking to God, asking for Him to explain why He loved me. Before college, I had never tried to understand what was so important about Jesus and
why He was the Word. I delved so deeply into reading and then rereading scripture that all other concerns just washed away. Then, my friend, Sam, whom I had not heard from in a while, invited me to the Campus House. He said he thought I would enjoy it. I hesitantly decided to go. I had no idea what an impact this group of God's people would have on my future.

I had been hanging out with friends at Campus House since midway through the Fall semester of 1988, and I was now getting ready to meet someone who was going to steal my heart. Penny had not been as involved at Campus House in the last semester, so I had not had the chance to encounter her. Now I was finally meeting her. For the last year, I had finally quit looking for the person who God had for me. But, as so often happens in life, you can find what you need when you are not looking for it.

Penny

One of my good friends had a massive crush on a new guy a Campus House. She had mentioned him to me several times. When I met Kendall at Campus House for the first time in the Fall of 1988, my first thought was that my friend was right; he was good-looking. He soon was part of our core group of friends. When he was not at Milligan, he was at Campus House, and we soon became good friends. It seemed he was always trying to get my attention. However, Kendall was also watching out for me. When I went out with a guy from Milligan, Kendall advised me not to go out with him, telling me that he had a bad reputation. Kendall was telling me the truth, not just being jealous. He was trying to protect me. When we went out to a restaurant as a group, Kendall always made sure he sat beside me to pick up my check because he knew I had little money. I knew Kendall was dating quite a bit as well. But, in my mind, we were friends first and foremost.

Kendall at Campus House small group. Also pictured: Amy Worrell.

Campus House was at its best that year. We had grown into a large group of students, and the house was open late with students playing cards and talking. After cooking together, we often went out an upstairs window to eat on the roof. We watched movies, played silly games, and played ping pong in the basement. But we were also delving into God's word, praying together, and talking to others about Christ on campus. Spending so much time together, I did begin to notice things about Kendall. He had a notebook where he wrote the scriptures he was studying. He was writing songs to God. He was genuinely seeking God, and, for me, that was the most attractive thing about him; his gray-green eyes notwithstanding. First, he asked me to go out with him as a friend. It was the first time I noticed his eyes. My heart was changing.

## Kendall

Penny has always had an enthusiasm for people. When she was talking to people, I noticed the importance she placed on listening to others. It was true too when I spoke with her. I guess it is why I was always trying to find ways to spend time with her. I often found myself dwelling on our conversations, how I enjoyed looking her in the eyes, and what I saw reflected back to me as we conversed. It did not take long for me to realize that my feelings for her were the reason.

The Campus House was working in security at the Tennessee Christian Teen Convention. A friend of ours was hanging around Penny, and I did not care much for it. I was jealous. As much as I hated that about myself, it did not seem like I could get rid of those feelings. Up to this point, I had never taken the time to let Penny know how I felt. She had heard it from our mutual friends, but mostly I was keeping my distance. I started praying that her feelings for me would change to more than just friendship.

Finally, I worked up the courage to ask her to dinner as friends. I wanted a chance to explain myself, so I figured a not-so-formal dinner at a local restaurant would do the job. While there, I opened my heart to her and told her that I cared deeply for her. I believe it was at this dinner that she decided to give me a chance. Not much longer after this, I decided to ask her out on an actual date. She said yes. I asked Sam if he would help me. I loaned Sam my tuxedo from the choir and began the preparations for our date.

Penny and I dressed up and drove to the location. Penny had no idea what was going on. When we arrived, Sam was there with everything set up and bubbly grape juice on ice. It could not have been more perfect and surreal until Sam dropped the two two-piece meal KFC boxes on the plates in front of us. I will never forget the smile on Penny's face.

Dinner at the gazebo, 1989

## Penny

Kendall asked me out on our first "real" date in April of 1989, eight months after we had first met. He borrowed his mom's car and brought me a dozen roses. He had even gotten his haircut for the occasion. I had no idea where we were going as we headed toward downtown Elizabethton. I was confused because there wasn't much downtown in the 1980s. We pulled up to a parking spot at the gazebo by the Doe River. Our good friend, Sam, was waiting on us in a tux. He had set a card table with fine china and silverware. He pulled out my folding chair and then sat across from me. As we waited, Sam brought out boxes of Kentucky Fried Chicken. One of the things that drew me to Kendall was his sense of humor. Even though he would always try to explain his jokes to me, I always got them. I got him. After our fine dining experience, we went for yogurt and then back to the Campus House, where we sat and talked for five hours. We were together as a couple after that day.

## Kendall

We had so many great friends at Campus House, friendships that have endured to this day. They are the kind of friendships that do not require constant maintenance; the next time you spend time with these people, it is like you have never been apart. Angela is one of these friends. One night we were downstairs at Campus House watching a movie with Angela and some other friends; one I had always loved as a child, but at the same time always creeped me out, Penny's childhood favorite, *Chitty-Chitty-Bang-Bang*. Before this night, Penny and I had never kissed, so why not make a move when the "child catcher" was on the loose in the quaint little Bulgarian village. All of our friends had left, and, as far as I could tell, our dear friend Angela was asleep across from us on the couch.

Later that weekend, we were at a friend's house for a party. We were playing a game called "Give me a smile." So far, just about everyone had given up a smile except me. It seemed that everyone thought it was impossible to make me smile. It's far from the truth as far as Angela was concerned. After all, she had a secret weapon because she tells me, "I wasn't asleep that night when you and Penny kissed for the first time." So, of course, I smiled.

## Penny

On the night I received prayer for my illness, Kendall was there with the other student leaders. Until this time, I was embarrassed about the muscle disease and calcinosis and did not share it with the guys I dated. I

34

made sure to hide the calcium deposits under clothing so that they wouldn't know. He knew the real me, and it did not matter; he still loved me. We prayed together as a couple. He shared the songs he was writing with me and the scriptures that inspired them. Not being a reader, he miraculously read through several books I had recommended. He even had to buy some new books for our campus minister because he tended to read with a highlighter in hand.

Sometimes I worried about his lack of independence from his parent's money. Kendall had anything he wanted at his fingertips with the use of his mother's credit card. When he had to take a semester off due to lack of funding, I encouraged him to get a job and an apartment of his own with a roommate to gain some experience managing his own money. Even then, I thought maybe we were headed toward marriage. I did not realize that it was also his credit that he was using, not just his parent's.

## Kendall

I had heard the phrase, "Money is the root of all evil." Unfortunately, when you are younger, it does not really sink in. While I was going to Milligan, I received a credit card application in my P.O. Box. I thought, "Wow, this is the coolest thing ever! Evidently, if they think it is a good idea to send me this, it must be a good idea to apply for it." So, I got it and started buying stuff on campus that I wanted, like food - a lot of food.

I also lacked direction. When I began college at Milligan, I was not sure what I wanted to do. I had never been a great student and did not care much for high school. My grades could not have been worse. I never studied, and I gave up way too quickly. I was the human equivalent of a car with four flat tires. It was sometime during my sophomore year of college that I began understanding and loving music.

I absorbed all the information from my music classes like a sponge. Music made sense to me, so I decided to declare as a Music major. I loved synthesizers, mixers, and studio gear. After taking quite a few of the required music classes, I discovered that the University of North Carolina at Asheville (UNC-A) had a Recording Arts degree. Unfortunately, I would have to be in Asheville while Penny was in Johnson City.

Kendall at his keyboard

# Chapter Five

**Faith *(noun)*: leads us to the heart of God** [4]

Hebrew 11:1

*Now faith is the substance of things hoped for, the evidence of things not seen.* (NKJV)

Penny

Kendall transferred to UNC-A in the Fall of 1989, my last year at ETSU. Asheville was on the other side of the mountain. I would miss him but knew he was close enough for us to travel back and forth. Kendall's first friend group at UNC-A was through Chi Alpha. As Kendall and I were part of the Christian Church, Chi Alpha was different for both of us. Looking back on it, especially as I am writing, I realize that I am the one who sought and asked for the filling of the Holy Spirit. However, Kendall was the one most drawn to this group. I guess I just loved a debate.

As far as I could see, the students in Chi Alpha knew what they believed, and they lived it well. However, they thought the evidence of being filled with the Holy Spirit was speaking in tongues. For one, that scared me, and two, I had just studied the Holy Spirit. I had seen the gift of tongues when receiving the Holy Spirit, but I did not see it in every passage. I did not see that *every* believer would speak in tongues. As I got to know them, I realized that debating theology was not important. Only their love

---

[4] Kyle Blevins. "*Why Faith, Hope, and Love Are So Important and Will Last Forever,*" *Crosswalk (blog), 2021.*

for Jesus was necessary, and they loved Him dearly. The fruit of the
Spirit (Gal 5:22-23) was evident in their lives. They became Kendall's best friends on campus, and I was glad he had them.

## Kendall

When I toured UNC-A, I found out that Dr. Kirby, the department head, was the keyboardist for Blondie back in the day. I thought that was pretty cool. I also found out that Robert Moog, the creator of the famous Moog synthesizer, was teaching electronics and digital music classes, and that thrilled me to no end. My first class with Dr. Moog was a challenge. His intelligence was beyond me. The next semester they revamped the class to a more hands-on approach, which helped me immensely. I had made a decision and had finally found peace in what I wanted to do.

## Penny

I graduated from ETSU with a Bachelor of Social Work in May 1990. During my college years, I was able to go to school, work full-time, and have a social life. It was truly a miracle. I had to use a handicapped tag to park closer to buildings, and I walked more slowly up steps than most students, but I could walk and climb steps! I had the energy to handle all the things I wanted to do. One of the things I wanted to do was see another part of the country. Before graduation, I received an offer to be the Unit Leader for a Christian Camp for Special Needs adults for the upcoming summer. The camp was outside of Boston, Massachusetts, in the small town of Groton. Leaving Kendall would be hard, but I booked my ticket with excitement and planned my next adventure.

My job for the camp would entail the supervision of eight counselors and 40 new campers each week. I was also responsible for the daily Bible teachings and music relevant to campers with Developmental Disabilities. I was also responsible for driving the campers in a forty-passenger bus daily to and from the lake. To say this was going to be a stretch for me is an understatement. Thankfully, I had the years of walking at ETSU behind me because, at camp, we never stopped. As soon as we arrived at the camp, we were required to take a three-mile trek through the woods. I had always been able to stop and rest when walking at school, but, this time, rest was not an option. I completed the hike tired but incredibly proud of myself.

Penny at Camp Grotonwood, MA

When I arrived at camp for training, a girl who had attended Asbury College in Kentucky was my roommate. We immediately connected. I was already missing my prayer times with my Campus House friends, so I was excited to realize God had sent me a new prayer partner. She was over a different part of the camp, but we would still get together weekly and on weekends to pray and encourage each other. We both had just graduated, we were dating someone we were not sure we should marry, and we were praying for God's will for our futures. I had faith that God would give me peace about what He wanted me to do. When I left home in June, I had been dating Kendall for a year and two months. I knew we were serious, but I wanted God's heart for our relationship.

Kendall made sure I did not forget him. It was the days before cell phones, and there was only one payphone on the campus. My co-workers were jealous of all the mail I received. Kendall sent me things as well. He sent me a Walkman portable tape player. (This was also the days before compact discs.) He sent me the Little Mermaid Soundtrack on tape because he knew I loved Disney movies. He sent me roses for my birthday. My friends from home told me he even went on the Delilah radio show to talk about me. He made sure I knew he loved me. As the summer continued, Mary and I continued to pray together, seeking God's will for our futures. By the time I was ready to come home at the end of August, I had peace.

Kendall

When Penny left for the camp in Groton, Massachusetts, she gave me a small case with all her jewelry in it to keep for her while she was gone. I always wondered why she did not just put it up. After receiving the case, I immediately thought of a plan. I had not given the future much thought, but it seemed that this summer would be different.

I had a ploy for asking her dad for permission to ask Penny to marry me. I had bought a new enclosure for some subwoofers I had purchased, which would sound great in the 1970's model Ford truck I was driving. However, the box was missing some screw holes to mount the subs. So, I called Penny's dad and asked if I could come by and use his drill for the holes. While I was there, I asked Jerry if it would be okay to ask Penny to marry me. He chuckled and said that he and Yvonne had figured that our marriage was inevitable.

I had decided that I would put the engagement ring in the small box of jewelry Penny had given me for safekeeping. So, when she opened the box, the ring would be there, and she would be dazed while I slid down on one knee and proposed to her. I had always had an issue with impulsive spending, but this was one of the few times I was taking my time. I looked at almost every jewelry store in Johnson City for a ring that I thought was worthy of Penny. I had created a calendar while Penny was gone in which I marked the days off until her return. It was now time, and I was ready.

June to August 1990

41

As I headed to the airport to pick her up, I was so excited! I was going to propose to my future wife. I was confident and terrified all at once. I was shaking with nervousness. I had already placed the ring in the jewelry box. I finally saw her, her hair had naturally turned blonde in the northern summer sun, and her voice was raspy due to lots of yelling and singing while she was at camp. There are few moments in life that you remember how something felt so precisely. I will never forget that hug. It was the kind of hug that replaced my missing heart, finally transplanting it back to its proper place.

As we left the airport, I continuously played what I was going to say over and over in my head. Finally, we arrived home, and I took all of her stuff upstairs to her bedroom. As she opened her suitcase looking for her necessities, she started throwing her dirty clothes on the floor. When she left the room to get a laundry basket, I pulled out the jewelry box and opened it to ensure the ring was still there. I thought to myself, "Nope this isn't the right time to do this. It's a mess in here, I'll pick a more appropriate time!" Of course, as I thought this, Penny walked by the door and saw her jewelry box and immediately came for it. She opened it and said, "What is this?" I dropped to one knee in the middle of the dirty clothes and said, "Umm... will you marry me?" I can only imagine the look on my face. Thankfully, she said yes.

Fall 1990

# Chapter Six

**Peace *(noun)*: state of security; freedom; mutual concord** (MW)

Philippians 4:6-7

*Be anxious for nothing, but in everything by prayer and petition, with thanksgiving, let your requests be made known to God; and the peace of God, which surpasses all understanding will guard your hearts and minds through Christ Jesus.* (NKJV)

Penny

Kendall was still in Asheville completing his degree. He was living in a cabin in Fletcher, NC, with some guys from Chi Alpha. Now that we were engaged, I decided I wanted to be as close to him as possible. So, I applied for a job in Fletcher with a nursing home. The administrator who interviewed me said that she had already decided to hire someone else, but another nursing home in the area also needed a social worker. So, I traveled to a mountain community in North Carolina, between Asheville and Johnson City, and interviewed for their Director of Social Services position. The Nursing Home Director offered me the position on the spot. I was twenty-two years old, right out of college, and I had a job. It was a little daunting to have so much responsibility, but I was determined to do well. It is funny to think that I started out making a fifteen thousand-a-year salary and was excited at how much money I was making. For a caseworker in the early '90s, that amount was the going rate. I found an apartment in an old house in downtown Asheville. My drive to work was beautiful. I had a view of the Grove Park Inn right by my apartment, and I drove through beautiful mountains on my way to work.

The cabin in Fletcher and the old truck

We enjoyed the nine months before our wedding. We explored Asheville together. We ate at our favorite restaurants, went to dollar movies, and explored the Blue Ridge Parkway. We made frequent trips on the old U.S. Route 19, back and forth to Johnson City. Usually, during these trips, Kendall would have to stop on the side of the road to write down a song on a napkin or a scrap piece of paper.

There was not an Independent Christian Church in Asheville at that time, so we visited many different denominations and churches. At one church, we knew the songs and sang out, but the people in front of us all turned around to stare. No one greeted us. We did not go back. The sermon was more like a lecture at another church we attended, and they did not use scripture during the entire service. Most places were not friendly, and it is hard to stay somewhere you do not feel welcome. We visited many churches before finally settling on a charismatic, non-denominational church in downtown Asheville where Kendall's Chi Alpha friends attended. It was different than anything I had ever experienced. He preached the Word of God, but I still did not agree with some of his theology. The church was not orderly with the gifts of the Spirit, and it left me feeling uncomfortable. It was a small church but friendly and welcoming. It was not home, but we had friends there, which helped.

Kendall and I had decided on two ministers to be a part of our wedding. So, for pre-marital counseling, we met with our Campus Minister from Campus House and his wife and also traveled to High Point, NC, to meet with Kendall's Youth Minister from his teenage years. We respected both marriages immensely. In High Point, we attended a day-long conference through Larry Burkett Ministries on Money Management.

I had struggled with guilt for most of my life. I felt guilty that my dad had to work so much because of my illness. I felt guilty that my mom had to stay with me in the hospital and be away from my sister. I felt guilty when my extended family called me an "angel" because I knew I was not even close. I even felt guilty when I received presents. So, with the wedding, I wanted it to cost as little as possible for my family. My Campus House friends were invaluable. I had a friend who would do the catering at cost. She also saved me the night before by volunteering to rent linens at a rental store so that I would not have to iron so many tablecloths the night before the wedding. Another friend I had asked to take the pictures for the wedding insisted on only charging for film and the development of the photos.

47

On May 18, 1991, Kendall and I were married at Grandview Christian Church. The church sanctuary was decked out in 1970's orange shag carpet already, so no matter what we had chosen for our décor, the carpet would outshine it. I had a few moments to myself, waiting on my turn to walk down the aisle. I was nervous, so as I waited, I used the time to pray. As I waited for my father, my Father God met me with a peace that passed all understanding. I felt His presence with me. I had no doubts. I would think about that peace often in the years to come.

Our wedding day, 1991

## Kendall

My parents and I had been to Edisto Beach several times at this point, and it had never rained, never even sprinkled, so from my viewpoint, this was the perfect location for our honeymoon. I kept telling Penny that our honeymoon would be exceptional based on the weather alone. "It's never rained while we've been there," I said, even after we hit heavy rain on our drive to Edisto. It kept raining hard, and I continued my insistence that the weather at Edisto Beach would be outstanding. I was so blessed and proud to be married to Penny that I even wanted to drive with my window down with my left hand out of the window to show the world my new ring.

Almost every day, it rained. And it rained and rained. We finally had a day without rain through the afternoon, which was the day I got sunburned. It was also the day the air conditioner quit working in the condo. We did enjoy the dining out, though there were only four restaurants on the island. Penny developed the symptoms of food poisoning after eating out one night and would not accept my offer to hold her hair while she threw up. That was also the night I knocked her drink in her lap, which was not great because I had left most of her clothes in Johnson City when I packed the car. We ate at a fine dining restaurant that I especially enjoyed. However, I did not enjoy the paired wine with my selection, so Penny drank mine too. She did not want to waste it. Since we had never been drinkers, I almost had to carry her out.

Thanks to my sunburn and no air conditioner, we decided to leave early and return home to Asheville, NC. You think when considering your life, "I hope everything works out perfectly. I hope nothing bad happens." But without the bad, there would be no good. Life would be dull. Just like our lives, our honeymoon was far from boring.

# Chapter Seven

**Surrender** *(intransitive verb)*: **to give oneself over to the power of another** (MW)

Hebrew 4:16

*Let us, therefore, come boldly to the throne of grace, that we may obtain mercy and find grace to help in time of need.* (NKJV)

Penny

At the end of the summer of 1991, we found an apartment in Weaverville, NC, halfway between UNC-A and my work. Kendall continued to attend UNC-A and found a job at a department store in Weaverville. We loved our new apartment. It was so much larger with a garage, a large kitchen and living room, a laundry room, and three bedrooms. It was in the basement of a ranch home and had a fenced-in backyard. Kendall used one of the bedrooms as his music room. It was cheaper than our one-bedroom apartment in the city. We adopted a cocker spaniel puppy and settled into living life together.

Kendall with our puppy, Laurel, in Weaverville, 1991

My job was becoming increasingly stressful. I worked sixty hours a week to keep up with visits to all one hundred and twenty residents plus documentation. We were a for-profit facility, so that meant I had pressure from our administrator to keep the beds full. My administrator had been nurturing and had provided me with an MSW for guidance on a consulting basis. Unfortunately, he was no longer with us, and the new administrator was harder to please.

During the months after our marriage, there was a marked increase in staph infections in the facility. I was still required to visit sick residents daily, so I had to be vigilant with hand washing. Since the latter part of college, I had been dealing with open wounds of broken calcium deposits. At some point in this epidemic at the facility, my left arm became infected. Because I had been on antibiotics for so many years, I had become immune to their benefit. After consulting with my doctor and trying several different antibiotics, they sent me to an infectious disease doctor.

By this time, I had been sick for a month. The infectious disease doctor immediately put me in the hospital on IV antibiotics. I was extremely ill with a high fever. I was in and out of consciousness, but Kendall was there beside me every time I woke up. The IV antibiotics did not work either. Finally, they decided to do surgery to remove the infection and calcium from my left bicep down to the crook of my arm through small incisions made up and down my arm. The surgery left holes that needed to be packed with new bandages daily.

After discharge, the nurse rolled me into the accounting office. I had had my own insurance and medical bills for almost a year, but nothing had prepared me for the invoice that awaited me in that office. They wanted a down payment. At this point, I had missed a month of work and had used all my sick days. Kendall and I only made eighteen thousand dollars a year with both our incomes when I was getting paid. Finally, I broke down in tears, and they let me leave without making a payment.

A great deal was expected of Kendall after I returned home. A home health nurse taught him how to pack my arm with bandages. He had to help me bathe and get dressed. It was very humbling for someone newly married, but I felt secure in Kendall's love. With everything, including school and work, he took excellent care of me. I continued to be out of work for another month. Thankfully, we discovered that our tax refund covered the debt we owed to the hospital and doctors. The experience made us dependent on each other and God.

Many of Kendall's friends had graduated, so we no longer had friends in the area. With his friends gone, we felt alone in the church. We did not have a connection apart from them. Even though the church knew about my illness, they seemed to forget about us. We were both working, and Kendall was going to school. It was a very lonely time. I spent much of my time studying scripture in the evenings while Kendall was at work. Thankfully, we both felt God's presence, and He was our source, not people or the church.

At my workplace, I was dealing with disputes with family members about combative patients. My administrator had given me an ultimatum to settle the issues but had not given me any guidance on how to get it done. I was still incredibly young without the wisdom of how to deal with the situations on my own. I had family members who were upset about the combative patient, and the aggressive patient's family was not willing to accept any solutions I offered. The disputes were so bad that people in the community started refusing to speak to me or even acknowledge me. I cried out to God daily and stayed in His word. I began to love the Psalms. I was surprised to see that the writers of the Psalms had similar feelings. I begged God for change - to move us from this area and this job.

I finally had come to a place in my walk with God, where I was ready to surrender. I decided to leave our lives in His hands because I realized His plans would be much better than any we could make. As a child, when I asked Jesus to be my Lord and Savior, I was baptized. At the time, I did not understand that knowing Him as my Savior and believing Him to be my Lord are two vastly different things. I honestly only understood that I wanted Jesus to save me. Now I was ready to make Him my Lord.

I am a list-maker, an organized planner at heart; however, I needed to give up that control to Him. I figured it would not hurt to make a list of everything dear to my heart and write out a prayer giving it all to Him. Ironic, I know. So, I did. I put everything I had been afraid of losing on the list. Kendall was at the top. I wanted to give it all to Him. The process of surrender would be something I would do over and over. I continue to surrender, sometimes daily, because I want nothing to stand in the way of my relationship with Jesus.

## Kendall

While Penny was struggling physically and at work, I was trying to finish school while also working. Thankfully, God was the center of our relationship. During my whole time in school, I had usually put assignments off until the last moment, except during my senior year at UNC-A. I submitted a request to write my Senior Humanities thesis on Computer Versus Human Creative Music. I started writing immediately. I wrote for several weeks finishing it several weeks ahead of time. The paper was one of the few A grades I had ever received.

During my last semester at UNC-A, I completed a senior recital and comprehensive exams. I successfully finished both and graduated in May 1992. During my last semester at UNC-A, I finally received in-state status and a refund of seven hundred dollars. I used part of the money to go to the Doulos Song Writing School in Nashville, an eye-opening experience. I always knew I had a better handle on the melody over lyrics, but I did not realize just how little I knew about the intricacies of songwriting.

Penny

Kendall's dream was to be a songwriter/audio engineer in Nashville, but we were unsure how to do that. So, we gave it to God. In June of 1992, my mom and I traveled to Nashville to meet Kendall during his last weekend at the songwriting school. While we were there, Mama and I had dinner with a couple from Murfreesboro who had attended our church in Johnson City. The wife was a service coordinator for children with disabilities. Because of my experience as a child with a disability, I wanted to learn about her job. She told me a preschool for children with disabilities was looking for a part-time social worker. It was a job share with another organization that served adults with disabilities. She gave me the contact information. I was excited about the possibilities.

Kendall came home enthusiastic about moving to Nashville. He was so excited about my possible job opportunity; he was ready to start packing, which, by faith, we did. We returned to Murfreesboro for an interview a few weeks later. I was called later that week with an offer. It was only seventeen thousand dollars a year, but it was still more than I had been making. I jumped at the opportunity. God had given us a way out, and we were moving to Nashville!

# Part Two

**Refused *(verb)*: to show or express unwillingness to do or comply with** (MW)

Nehemiah 9:17

*They refused to obey,*
*And they were not mindful of Your wonders*
*That You did among them...*
*But You are God,*
*Ready to pardon,*
*Gracious and merciful,*
*Slow to anger,*
*Abundant in kindness,*
*And did not forsake them.* (NKJV)

# Chapter Eight

**Diligence *(noun)*: steady, earnest, and energetic effort** (MW)

Hebrews 11:6

*But without faith it is impossible to please God, for he who comes to God must believe that He is, and that He is a rewarder of those who diligently seek Him.* (NKJV)

## Penny

Kendall and I fell in love with the Nashville suburb of Franklin, TN. Franklin has a beautiful, old downtown area with a small-town feel, close to Nashville. Many Christian and country artists lived in Franklin, and it had several music studios. I was working in Murfreesboro and traveled a small, scenic highway from Franklin to Murfreesboro. Kendall got a job working as a server at Cracker Barrel in the evenings to leave his schedule open for internships in music studios during the day. It meant he was working all the time, but it also meant he was following his dream, so I was happy.

## Kendall

I had contacted a friend of mine whom I had gotten to know at Appalachian Christian Camp in Unicoi, TN. He had moved to Nashville to pursue a career in the music business and had been successful in the area as a recording engineer. I contacted him and started going to some of his recording and mixing sessions to get an idea of what was going on locally. I loved what I saw. I heard that there was an internship available at Hummingbird Productions, a studio that created commercial music. I worked there whenever I could. After that, I worked an internship at Classic Recording. During these times, I had the honor of meeting quite a few well-known musicians and artists. I enjoyed interning, but I was not getting paid, and I was working days and nights. It cut down on my time with Penny.

## Penny

I was happy with my job. I loved my clients and my families. In helping families deal with the trials of illness and disability, I felt that I was fulfilling a calling. Even though I was only twenty-four, my adult clients with developmental disabilities treated me like a mother. I was responsible for their medication, doctor's appointments, SSI (Supplemental Security Income), and shopping. God gave me godly women who were between ten and thirty years older than I was to offer me wisdom and guidance so I did not feel alone.

Because of our experience in Asheville, we did not want to return to a charismatic church. Instead, God led us to Franklin Christian Church, a new church in the Franklin community. It was small with only one hundred and fifty people, but on our first visit, we were made welcome. We were invited to the church picnic right after church that Sunday. While there, we met a young couple who would later become life-long friends. He was an audio engineer, musician, and fellow "trekie." She was a "kindred spirit," and we had fun shopping in craft markets and local shops and serving in the women's ministry together. Because Kendall worked most holidays, and their families were on the coast, we took turns having Thanksgiving at each other's homes. It was wonderful to have new friends and a church family. I now had "family" away from home. New friends surrounded me, but for some reason, God felt extremely far away.

As I have said, throughout all my childhood, I remember constantly dealing with feelings of guilt. I learned the concept of grace but apparently did not feel it applied to me. I felt like a liar, and sometimes, to hide my inadequacies, I became a liar. As a child, because of my illness, I did not get into trouble. However, as I grew, I felt I needed to work harder and be better to maintain what others thought of me. I lived for praise, but it was a high that was short-lived. I always cared about what others thought and often thought God was disappointed in me.

So, as a newly married woman joining the first church since my childhood, I threw myself into what I knew, serving. I volunteered for everything. I worked in the nursery and made Kendall work with me. I helped in the women's ministry. I taught a Sunday night class of four and five-year-old children. I washed communion cups and took meals to sick people. My minister even noticed and had a talk with me about learning to say no. However, no matter how hard I worked, I was not getting closer to God.

## Kendall

After moving to Franklin, it did not take me long to find big-ticket items that I wanted, keyboards, speakers, etc. So, I started using my credit card again. I have always felt that debt is a sin for me. Debt is not God's best for us. Debt is a hole that people dig quickly and struggle to find a way to climb out.

## Penny

Not long after our move to Franklin, I discovered something I did not know about my husband. I knew I had come into our marriage debt-free and that he had not, but we had attended pre-marriage counseling specifically about debt. My parents were tithers, and I wanted us to be a giver too. I started finding receipts. I discovered Kendall had bought a keyboard and was storing it at our church (yes, at our church) to hide it from me. I had recently paid off a credit card, but then I received a bill showing more charges. We talked about it as a couple. I was angry, and he tried to understand my anger, but that was as far as it went. I was his only accountability. In my naivety, I thought talking out the problem had solved the problem. I had many friends, but I did not want to share Kendall's deception with anyone. I did not fully understand how it would eventually affect our lives.

During times of trouble, I had always felt closer to God. I did not know what else to do, so I talked to the silence. I read more books, read my Bible, and went to more Bible studies, but I still did not feel His presence. A friend at work told me that sometimes God is silent or feels far away, but He is always close, even if we cannot feel Him. God was there and had much more to teach me. He had plans. I cried out to God and asked him to send me a prayer partner, someone who understood my deep desire for more of God, someone to pray with me about my marriage. But, until He sent someone, I would continue to do what I knew to do.

Galatians 6:9

*And let us not grow weary while doing good, for in due season we will reap if we do not lose heart.* (NKJV)

Until this time, I had split my time between my adult clients with disabilities and young families with children ages birth to three with disabilities. Both were part-time. I loved my adult clients, but the young families were my heart. Middle Tennessee State University changed my position with young families to a full-time position, so, with some sadness, I left my adult clients behind. We were both in jobs we loved, so now I was ready for more. Isn't that the way it always is? We are a society of wanting more, and we want it now. However, God is a God of process. It is more about the journey. I had so much to learn.

## Kendall

I had worked for free for studios for the last two years. Because there were so many students interning in Nashville without pay, finding an actual job in the industry was difficult. I finally had an opportunity to interview for a job in the entertainment industry. It was the first time I had been able to use what I had learned so far in live audio engineering in an actual job. I was offered a job as a stagehand on the General Jackson Showboat and accepted. Although I was usually backstage, I was able to help set up sound gear for shows done on the upper decks and aided the show's audio engineer in set-ups and sound checks. The following year I was offered a job as the audio technician for shows within Opryland Theme Park.

## Penny

So, the things I wanted next were a house and a baby. Kendall was on board for the house, but the baby not so much. So, I went with what he was giving me. Kendall agreed to start our journey to home-ownership by attending a first-time home-buyers class at our bank. The home-ownership course helped us be informed and took away some of our fear of going into a possible mortgage. Our bank did not approve us for a loan, but we did not give up. Our realtor, a friend from our church, recommended an agent at a mortgage company. The mortgage lender pre-approved us for a loan immediately. However, the loan was so minuscule; we were unsure we could find a house in that price range.

Our realtor was more familiar with the large houses in Franklin, so looking at such tiny houses was a bit of a stretch for her. Thankfully, Kendall and I both have the vision to see what something can become. We found a home in LaVergne between Nashville and Murfreesboro. It was eleven hundred square feet, smelled strongly of smoke, had old, dark brown shag carpeting and red, cow-print wallpaper. Our realtor wanted to leave as soon as we walked in the door. However, Kendall and I saw all that it offered. We thought it was luxury. We made an offer of sixty-three thousand dollars, and the owners accepted the contract. Unfortunately, the owner had cancer, so we negotiated when occupancy could occur and then gave our notice to the apartment complex.

The former owners had been paying us rent since just after we had closed on the house. We loaded the truck and drove to the house on the day we had negotiated to move in. When we arrived, they were still in residence. They said we were wrong about the move-in day. We talked to both realtors. The old couple was not moving out. Since she had cancer and was currently struggling with her health, we did not push but renegotiated another move-in date in a month.

Sitting in that truck, in the driveway of a house we owned, we did not know what we were going to do. Yet, looking back, I am still astounded by how God took care of us. Kendall and I had become friends with one of my co-workers and her husband. Faith had not come into our relationship at all, but they were the ones who took us in when we had nowhere to go. It was their idea. They had bought a house in Nashville, so they were also in the process of moving. We moved all our belongings into their living room in Murfreesboro. They would take nothing from us and treated us, and our dog, like family. When we finally moved into our house, Kendall immediately started ripping out carpet, tearing down wallpaper, and putting new layers of paint on the walls to cover the smell of smoke. After the dust settled and remodeling was over, the house was just as we had pictured.

Kendall in front of our house in LaVergne, 1994

# Chapter Nine

**Pilgrimage *(noun)*: a journey** (MW)

Psalm 84:5-7

*Blessed is the man whose strength is in You, whose heart is set on pilgrimage. As they pass through the Valley of Baca, they make it a spring: the rain also covers it with pools. They go from strength to strength; each one appears before God in Zion.* (NKJV)

Penny

Before we moved to our new home in LaVergne, a life-long friend of mine, who lived in Johnson City, called to tell me that she and her husband were moving to Nashville. Immediately, I knew that God had not forgotten my earlier prayer. He was answering my prayer and sending me a prayer partner. Ginger believed in being filled to overflowing with the Holy Spirit. She prayed with power and authority, and her faith was evident to everyone she met. Ginger moved to Nashville along with her husband and her baby daughter. She was a stay-at-home, new mom, and I was working; but we came together once a week to eat, pray, and spend time together.

During this time, Ginger started talking with me about the "baptism of the Holy Spirit." I told her my experience in college asking for the filling of the Holy Spirit (Acts 4:31 NKJV) and my belief that we receive and are sealed with the Holy Spirit when we first believe (Eph.

1:13 NKJV) and are baptized (Matt. 3:11 NKJV). We started studying the scriptures concerning the Holy Spirit. I decided there was still more to receive from Him. The Greek word translated as filled in Ephesians 5:18 indicates being filled to capacity. In Titus 3:5-6 it says, *"...according to His mercy He saved us, through the...renewing of the Holy Spirit, whom He poured out on us abundantly through Jesus Christ our Savior."* (NKJV) I wanted the fullness of God. I wanted the abundance.

To baptize means to immerse. As a child, I was baptized: a physical representation of being buried with Christ and rising with Him. Now, I wanted spiritual immersion in His presence. Submission is always a little bit scary. Our God is awesome and powerful, but He has also said, in Hebrews 4:15-16, that *"We do not have a High Priest who cannot sympathize with our weaknesses, but was in all points tempted as we are, yet without sin. Let us, therefore, come boldly to the throne of grace that we may obtain mercy and find grace to help in our time of need."* (NKJV) He loves us, and He knows our fears. He has made it possible for us to approach Him with boldness. He will take care of us in any place He takes us.

When you ask Him for something, God will meet you where you are. So, I believe that when I asked the Holy Spirit to fill me, He filled me right up to the top. He was not the One holding back. I was. Now, I was wanted to be completely submerged, meet Him moment-by-moment, submit to His will for my life, and be led by His Spirit. Because we are all individuals, I believe He will teach us and lead us in a way we can understand. He loves us as individuals unconditionally, exactly where we are. He knows our personalities and our weaknesses and loves us anyway. He gives us exactly what we need, how we need it, and at the moment we need it. James 4:8 promises that if we draw near to God, He will draw near to us. (NKJV)

The words I have used - surrender, sealed, filled, baptized - are foreign to some, and others may think of them as the same thing. To me, they brought order and showed a process of how God was dealing with me. Because I was fearful of the unknown, He led me slowly. When I asked for the filling of the Spirit, I wanted help doing what He wanted me to do. When I surrendered to Him, I finally understood I wanted Him to be the Lord of my life. When I asked to be baptized by the Spirit, I was ready to be immersed in His presence and whatever that brought with it. I believe He did as I asked because I was a changed person with fruit to prove it.

Ginger told me she could pray with power only because she prayed the word of God, which is power. The Holy Spirit helped me to dive into the word of God again without using books or Bible studies to help me. I asked Him to stop me when I was reading if He wanted me to notice something. So, when I was reading, I started receiving promptings to stop and go back and reread it, sometimes over and over, until I understood what God was saying. I started writing down scripture to pray out loud. Because I was praying it out loud, the scripture went into my heart. Having the scripture in my heart and mind was one way I could hear God's voice. I had never read the Bible in its entirety. When I started reading this time, I marked each chapter I read, noting the year. I read the entire Bible for the first time and had a mark to remind myself that I had completed it. Romans 10:17 says, *"Faith comes by hearing and hearing by the word of God."*

(NKJV) Because I was studying the word of God and listening to the word of God, my faith was increasing.

God was constantly giving me opportunities to increase my faith. When I went to my Obstetrician to talk to her about my desire to get pregnant, she spoke with me about several issues. Although she did not believe the calcium was in my uterus or organs, they were all around the uterus, so she was unsure of its effect on my ability to carry a baby. The calcium deposits were still open and seeping, so my risk for infection was also a concern. Despite these concerns, by faith, we began purposely trying to have a baby. Ginger and I covered it with prayer.

Once we moved to LaVergne, Kendall and I had continued to attend the same church; however, now we were traveling forty-five minutes each way by backroads. Ginger invited us to her "cell group," a small group of people from her church who met together for Bible Study, worship, and fellowship. We met everyone for the first time at a Halloween party. At the time, we were the only childless couple, but they immediately embraced us. The group leader was a musician and songwriter, so Kendall was excited to discuss what he loved most. Soon, we were attending the cell group weekly and attending the church weekly.

Our new friends believed that the Holy Spirit was still doing everything He had been doing in the New Testament. Most of all, they desired to make disciples of Christ and be obedient to the call upon their lives. The church consisted of smaller groups with group leaders who had the church's vision for the group. The group resembled the Acts 2 church more than any I had ever experienced up to that point. They became our family. We lived life together. We spent time together, ate together, studied the Bible together, prayed for each other, praised God together, took communion together, and met one another's needs. It was an amazing time.

It seemed it took longer than I expected to get pregnant. Then, in October 1995, nine months after we stopped using birth control, I found out I was expecting. Soon fear reared its ugly head as I became fearful of miscarriage. My doctor did an ultrasound every three months because of the calcium and muscle disease. She was confident everything was fine, but I continued to worry. My metabolic specialist wanted to take advantage of the situation and removed dairy from my diet in hopes that the baby would take the calcium from the deposits. I worried that not eating calcium would hurt the baby. Kendall had a fear of losing me to death in childbirth. There was quite a bit of anxiety surrounding us. In my Bible study, God led me to Exodus 23:25-26, which said, "So *you shall serve the Lord your God, and He will bless your food and your water. And I will take sickness away from the midst of you. No one shall suffer miscarriage or be barren in your land; I will fulfill the number of your days.*" (NKJV) In my mind, that covered it. It was another test of faith for me. If I became fearful, I said it out loud. If Kendall spoke fear, I said it out loud. God met me on His word. It helped that Ginger was now pregnant, and I had my small group to love and support me.

Baby shower with cell group, 1996

# Chapter Ten

**Shaken *(verb)*: to cause to move; to experience a state of instability** (MW)

Hebrews 12: 26-27

*He has promised, saying, "Yet once more I shake not only the earth, but also heaven." Now this, "Yet once more," indicates the removal of those things that are being shaken, as of things that are made, that the things which cannot be shaken may remain.* (NKJV)

Penny

It seems that as soon as Ginger arrived, God called her and her husband elsewhere. It may seem arrogant that I felt God sent her to Nashville to be with me, but at the time, it seemed that way. I would be eternally grateful for that time in our lives. When they left, we still had our small group family, and they surrounded and took care of us. The women were all mothers and helped me to understand what I was experiencing. I spent many nights and weekends in their homes watching movies, eating, and swimming. They fed me, taught me, and prayed for me.

I continued to work right up until the day I delivered. My mom had come to stay with me early so she would be with me when I went into labor. We called my dad and sister, and Ginger, who was also very pregnant at the time, and they all came as well. They had plenty of time to drive to Nashville and wait after they got to the hospital. After seventeen hours of labor, Mackenzie Ryanne Cochran was finally born. Because of damage to my muscles caused by the muscle disease, I had trouble pushing. So, I had lots of help from the two nurses who got on top of me to help deliver her. She was beautiful and big! Mackenzie weighed eight pounds and ten ounces and was the largest baby in the nursery. Kendall was immensely proud.

Mackenzie's Dedication Day, 1996

Thankfully, my mom and sister stayed with me because I felt like a failure from day one. I had trouble figuring out the whole nursing thing. Because Mackenzie was not getting any nourishment, she developed jaundice and lost one pound and eleven ounces in the first week. Thankfully, she had been a large baby; however, now she was not. I also started getting depressed and cried constantly. I went to a lactation specialist and took her to see the pediatrician every other day. The lactation specialist told me I was doing everything correctly; however, Mackenzie would turn her head, hold her little hands up in the air, and scream, as if to say, "no, I don't want to eat." That should have been my first hint that she was going to be a strong-willed child. The pediatrician had me add formula to her diet. She would not take a bottle either so, every time I tried to nurse her, I gave her formula that I fed her through a dropper. Again, I am thankful I serve a gracious God. I cried out to Him in my distress, asking Him to make her want to eat. Finally, one morning she woke up and started nursing.

After my mom and sister went back home, I sat in a chair holding Mackenzie and crying for a whole day. Thankfully, my small group friends did not leave me alone. They surrounded me. They brought food, sat, talked with me while I nursed, and helped me gain confidence in my new role. It is exhausting having a new baby, but I could not imagine being away from her. In my job, I often worked with children in their daycares and was not happy with what I saw happening. I could not find a place that I trusted to keep my child. So even though I had a fantastic job that I genuinely loved, we decided that I should stay home. After my six weeks of maternity leave, I turned in my notice at work. Unfortunately, my job was the one with insurance and the one that was most stable. It put tons of pressure on Kendall and led to some tough decisions, but it was the decision we made. I cannot look back in regret because the decision to stay home molded me into who I am and caused me to lean harder on God. I was also able to spend precious time with my baby, and I could never regret that.

I enjoyed every moment I spent as a stay-at-home mom. It felt like what I was supposed to do. But, just as I had been with every part of my life, Mackenzie was on a schedule. I arranged her schedule for the day around when she had awakened to eat in the morning. She ate with the same amount of time between feedings. In between nursing, I moved her around all day. She had floor time, belly time, swing time, nap time. And so, our lives together commenced.

## Kendall

When we moved to our house in Lavergne, we decided to get a new MacIntosh computer. I wanted it to help me create and notate music. While working at Cracker Barrel, one of my co-workers told me that they had recently gotten internet service because it had become available. Even though I did not know much about it, I was immediately intrigued and decided to get it. When I opened the browser for the first time, and web pages came up, it blew my mind. I thought it would be text-based, and graphics would cost more. However, it did not take long to realize what was available on the internet. Looking at pornography on the internet was extremely easy. I was about to get myself into deep spiritual and psychological trouble quickly. I had opened the door to temptation in more areas than just money. Spending money and giving in to the temptation of pornography had become my way of dealing with stress. I believe that each time I involved myself, the next time came easier.

Romans 8:13 *For if you live according to the flesh, you will die, but if by the Spirit you put to death the misdeeds of the body, you will live.* (NKJV)

## Penny

I hate to say I did not even realize how hard this time was for Kendall. We only had one car, so one day while I was in it by myself, I found some unfamiliar credit card bills in Kendall's name from an unknown post office address. I had always been in charge of the finances. I would be upset, but we always covered it. We tithed and knew God would take care of us, but I honestly thought Kendall had changed and that he was over the compulsion to spend. The bills proved that I had been wrong. Then our mortgage payment went up. When we took out the home loan, we did not fully grasp what an adjustable-rate mortgage was. After two years, the amount went up by fifty dollars per month. It does not sound like much, but it scared us.

## Kendall

Rumors began to surface during the summer of 1997 that Gaylord, the park's owner, was considering selling or demolishing the theme park. When the summer of 1997 ended, I was unwilling to take a decrease in pay to go back to being a stagehand again. All the audio engineer and tech jobs on the General Jackson would be going to those with seniority. So, instead of being demoted, I chose to take a job driving for Papa John's Pizza. It paid even less money than the stagehand job. Why do we do things like that? I soon became a part-time manager for Papa John's and drove delivery on the weekends. Soon after, my dad brought up the possibility of moving back to Northeast Tennessee to work with him.

## Penny

Kendall started talking about moving back to East Tennessee. My first reaction was excitement, but of course, soon worry and doubt crept in. I knew God wanted to strip away all the fear and insecurity that dominated my life. I continued in His word and asked the Holy Spirit to direct my study. He gave me 2 Timothy 1:7, which says, *"For God has not given us a spirit of fear, but of power and of love and of sound mind"*(NKJV) and Philippians 4:6-7, *"Be anxious for nothing, but in everything by prayer and supplication, with thanksgiving let your requests be made known to God and the peace of God, which surpasses all understanding, will guard your hearts and minds through Christ Jesus."*(NKJV) I kept

77

these words before my eyes, spoken out of my mouth and in my heart continuously.

With every worry that arose, I started with bringing it to God. He always met me. Concerning the house, I had some grief. I loved our house where I had brought home our little one. God gave me a scripture for that as well. Psalm 84:3-4 says, *"Even the sparrow has found a home and the swallow a nest for herself, where she may lay her young - even your altars, O Lord of hosts, my King, and my God. Blessed are those who dwell in Your house, they will be praising You."* (NKJV)

I was sad to leave our friends in the small group and, for the first time, I had a dream. I usually do not remember my dreams, and this felt like a "God" dream, so it got my attention. When I shared the dream with the small group, the leader confirmed that it lined up with the plans they had already talked about to stop being group leaders. In addition, one of the other members stated they were moving to another city, and Ginger and her family had already left. So, our time with our friends was coming to an end.

In February 1997, we put the house on the market. When I prayed about what we should ask for the house, the figure seventy-eight thousand came to mind. I felt it was too much, and my extended family thought it was too much since we had only paid sixty-three thousand dollars when we bought it. I left it in God's hands. We found a realtor from our church to help us. After seeing the house, he told us he wanted to list it for seventy-eight thousand, nine hundred dollars. God gave me peace that I did not need to do anything; He would sell it. We were struggling to meet our budget. However, every month, we continued to tithe and trust God, and He met our needs.

Waiting can be challenging. We had accepted two offers below the seventy-eight thousand, but both contracts fell through when they could not get a loan. Once again, I decided to make a list of the things I needed to surrender to God. I made plans to join Kendall's mom at the beach. Instead of worrying, I decided to stand on His word, believing that He would do it. A few days before I left, we received an offer for seventy-eight thousand dollars. We accepted, and the closing was set for June first.

We had a plan even before we sold the house. Kendall's parents had told us he could work for his dad's company, and we could live in the farmhouse in Limestone. Kendall had received management experience at Papa Johns and on the General Jackson. We were excited about the opportunity to join the family business. However, moving back home would require more patience and humility than I realized.

# Chapter Eleven

**Thorns *(noun)*: sharp, impeding processes causing irritation (**MW)

Matthew 13:22-23

*As for what was sown among thorns, this is the one who hears the word, but the cares of the world and the lure of wealth choke the word, and it yields nothing. But as for what was sown on good soil, this is the one who hears the word and understands it, who indeed bears fruit..."* (NRSV)

Penny

A month and a half after the move, in July 1997, I was invited to an Aglow meeting, an interdenominational women's fellowship. The meeting was incredible, but a woman I had never met came up to me after the meeting. She said the Lord had given her a word for me. She told me that the Lord told her I would go down a thorny path, but He would settle me in the end. The year before Ginger had given me 1 Peter 5:10, which says, *"But may the God of all grace, who called us to His eternal glory by Christ Jesus, after you have suffered a while, perfect, establish, strengthen and settle you."* (NKJV) I was looking forward to the perfect, establish, strengthen, and settle part. The word also led me to Matthew 13:22, which says, *"Now he who received seed among the thorns is he who hears the word, and the cares of this word and the deceitfulness of riches choke the word, and he becomes unfruitful."*

(NKJV) So, not a fun word to receive, but everything within me felt it was the truth. I had scripture to confirm it.

Thankfully, we moved with eleven thousand dollars in the bank. We would need every penny. Immediately, I let the chaos of our new life overtake me. I did not spend time with God for two weeks after the move except for quick prayers sent up asking for Him to help me deal with our new life. So many things were overwhelming us: the house, our money situation, finding a church, and extended family all had a part in increasing our anxiety. The farmhouse was in the middle of a remodel on the inside. It was full of dust and scary things for a mother with a baby just starting to walk. Mackenzie slept in a pack-n-play for months so we could move her bed around.

Mackenzie and Laurel in the kitchen of the farmhouse, 1998

## Kendall

I started working with my dad at his business, Southeastern Window and Siding, immediately after moving to East Tennessee. I wanted to put his business on a computer and help with workflow, but he wanted me to learn the sales side of things. I thought that with proper training, I might be able to do it. So, he sent me to Michigan for sales training, which for me was pretty stressful. Before I went to Michigan, I knew I did not like sales, but the training class confirmed it. I was able to sell some windows to several people but was not happy. I was not making enough to support our family.

## Penny

Kendall was only making a thousand dollars a month. Because of our low income, I was able to get food for Mackenzie on the Women, Infants, and Children (WIC) Supplemental Nutrition Program and Medicaid insurance through the TennCare program. We still had some credit card debt and Kendall's student loans, but we were not making enough to pay the bills, so we ended up using our savings from the sale of the house. Kendall was feeling discouraged working for his dad. He was hoping to be a manager, but his dad wanted him in sales. He decided to leave the family business to ease the stress of his relationship with his dad. However, once Kendall stopped working for his dad, his dad started asking for rent. We were not able financially to pay rent, so that fell to the wayside.

After Kendall stopped working for his dad, he started a job at the local TV station. However, he was making the same amount his dad paid, so it did not help us, even though he liked it better. He was soon let go. He went back to his old stand-by, Papa Johns, but was not getting the hours he needed. Next came a customer service job at a local company. He soon lost that job as well. In the last seven months of our lives, Kendall had worked four jobs. It was hard on me but even harder on Kendall.

Finding a church was also stressful. My home church and Kendall's were both forty-five minutes away in opposite directions. We wanted to find a church like our church in Nashville, but we were not sure it was possible. We started visiting churches but just could not find one that felt like home. Dava Lee, a former teacher and friend, had invited me to her Bible study, so we decided to visit her church as well. At the service, the pastor's sermon was almost identical to the last one we had heard in Nashville. I felt that God was telling me that this was the church. After that first service, another friend introduced us to the pastor and his wife. She was the praise and worship minister and recruited Kendall to play the keyboard. As always, we started serving almost as soon as we walked in the door.

I have to say: it was a lot harder living close to family than I thought. For one, I had changed. We chose a church that was not the home church for either of us. Our choice did not make either of our mothers happy. When we lived in Nashville and came home to visit, we always spent all of our time with family. Now we needed our own family time, but I struggled with trying to make everyone else happy. In case you are wondering, it's impossible. Kendall had worked in his dad's business; we lived in one of his family's homes and drove one of their cars. It was easy to be offended, feel manipulated, or just upset by the expectations that we thought we could not meet. I needed to surrender my feelings daily, but instead, I found myself constantly struggling against God and my emotions. I never felt like I was doing enough for Him or being enough for others. Kendall's grandmother, who I adored, came to live with us for three months in September 1997. She was such a blessing to us, and I cherish the time I had with her, but it was someone else to care for, and sometimes it was hard.

Looking back, God did some amazing things for us during this time. In 1997 we only made twelve thousand dollars according to our taxes, yet we paid every bill on time. We always had food. We had a roof over our heads. We still had some savings from the house in LaVergne. He gave me time with my baby by allowing me to stay home. Kendall had a car accident that totaled his dad's car, but he came away from it without any injury, and God gave us the money for another vehicle after the accident.

Some of the things I thought I was conquering while in Nashville crept back in - guilt, fear, gossip, negativity, apathy, a need for control, lack of forgiveness, and even lying. When we take our eyes off Jesus and instead focus on the circumstances around us, sin will return. However, God continued to speak to me the entire time we were in East Tennessee in the middle of the chaos and the strife. When I drew near to Him, He always drew near to me. (James 4:8 NKJV) When I was alone with Him or in a Bible Study or church service, I learned from Him and heard His voice. I was just having a hard time walking it out the rest of the time. I cried out to Him asking Him to teach me how to stay with Him continuously, not just when praying or spending time in His word.

Because I was reading and understanding scripture only recently, there was much of the Word of God that I was only beginning to understand. God started pointing out the word "Abide" to me throughout the book of John. John 15:5 says, *"I am the vine, you are the branches. He who abides in Me, and I in him, bears much fruit; for without Me you can do nothing."* (NKJV) I wanted to bear fruit and be productive for His Kingdom. I wanted to love as He loves. The word abide means "to remain, to dwell, to stay." So, I determined that I needed to stay as close to Him as possible and remain there. Abiding in Him was easier said than done.

At the beginning of 1998, I had struggled with quite a bit of sickness. I had had the flu and infections in the calcium deposits in my arms. As we entered spring, I developed an infection in the calcium deposits in my knee. Antibiotics by mouth were not working this time, so my doctor soon put me in the hospital with a high fever. Unfortunately, only Mackenzie had insurance. With help from the hospital social worker, Kendall applied for emergency Medicaid, and I was approved.

I believed with all my heart that God was able to heal me completely from the calcium deposits. I just did not understand why he did not. The church I was in taught that God would heal you if you had enough faith. I believed it and prayed earnestly for it. So, in my mind, if I was not healed, then I must not have enough faith. So, of course, this belief became part of my guilt complex and a stumbling block for my faith.

Psalm 27:13-14

*I would have lost heart, unless I had believed that I would see the goodness of the Lord in the land of the living. Wait on the Lord; be of good courage, and he shall strengthen your heart; wait, I say, on the Lord!* (NKJV)

Soon after my release from the hospital in April, I was looking for something in a desk drawer and found a credit card bill for fifty-two hundred dollars. I was devastated. Kendall had been lying to me again. As I began to sob and cry out to God, Ginger called to tell me she was in town. She wanted me to meet her. I was blown away by the love I received from my Savior. As we talked and prayed, God gave us a plan of attack. Kendall and I started going to Pastoral and financial counseling at our church. Kendall continued to play in the praise band at church. I continued to pray over him and love him. Unfortunately, Kendall could not be truly accountable to anyone. To be accountable, you have to be truthful. While we were still in counseling, I discovered he had spent two thousand more in two months. We were negative in our checking and savings accounts. Up to this point, we had not paid Kendall's dad any money to stay in the farmhouse. Now Kendall's dad was asking for rent to be paid by July.

## Kendall

After giving the church our first computer, I went behind Penny's back and purchased a new Fujitsu Laptop. It was only the beginning of what I would spend behind her back. My greed for money led to coveting things; coveting things led me to pursue the desires of my body. But it did not always flow in one direction; it was more like waves in a bowl. They bounced back and forth, waves to the side, then back to the center. Some of the mightiest forces on the planet involve waves. When you go out into the ocean, you can get in serious trouble quickly. My lust for money and things co-mingled with the lust of my flesh and pornography. I was getting into serious trouble.

## Penny

I knew that if we were going to make it, we could only do it with God being first in our lives. As God led me, I started learning to say "no" and decided to let go of several of the volunteer jobs I did at church. I again wrote out all of the scriptures I wanted to confess daily over myself and my family. I posted Mackenzie's scriptures in her room so that I could pray them over her before bed. I made it a priority to spend time studying my Bible daily. Mackenzie and I started having worship time at home. I knew God was our only hope. Besides writing down scripture, I went back to keeping a journal. I wrote about my hurts, my fears, and my prayers. I wrote down what He had blessed me with that day, the scriptures He gave me for the day, and when He convicted me of something. I told God that I would give up my dream of ever having a home of my own if He would just restore Kendall. God even gave me a couple of visions for the future, which I wrote down and kept close to my heart. The visions included Kendall and Johnson City. They gave me hope.

I tended to hold onto my sins even after I had confessed them to God. He still had so much to teach me. Romans 8:1-2 says, *"There is no condemnation to those who are in Christ Jesus, who do not walk according to the flesh but according to the Spirit. For the law of the Spirit of life in Christ Jesus has made me free from the law of sin and death."* (NKJV) God had to do quite a bit of breaking so that He would truly live through me. Part of the breaking for me was confessing what I had done. I had to acknowledge my sin to God, but God also asked me to admit what I had done to other people. My biggest sin was pride and wanting to look good to others, so confessing my sin to others was mortifying. I began to realize that surrendering all the things and people I loved was not enough. He wanted all of me. He wanted me to lay down myself.

# Chapter Twelve

**Little by Little *(adverb)*: by small degrees, gradually** (MW)

Exodus 23:29-30

*I will not drive them out from before you in one year, or the land would become desolate and the animals would multiply against you. Little by little I will drive them out from before you, until you have increased and you possess the land.* (NRSV)

Penny

In July 1998, Kendall received a job offer with Ryan's Steakhouse as a manager. He would be going to training in Greer, SC, for a month, and then assigned to a store, possibly in another state. Kendall's dad wanted to sell the house as soon as possible, and he wanted us to move before Kendall completed his training. The logical place for Mackenzie and me to go was to my parent's home, but I felt God was telling me I would be staying with my friend Donna's family from church. So, I left it up to God. I asked Him to have Donna ask me to stay with them if that was His plan. Without any prompting on my part, Donna called.

It was soon evident that one of the reasons I was at Donna's instead of my parent's home was that He wanted me to do what He said first and not be moved by guilt or trying to please others. Unfortunately, my family did not understand. I had to separate myself from my mother's emotions and my mother-in-law's daily phone calls. Keeping everyone happy was not His goal for me. I needed to put Him first and listen to His instructions. It was extremely difficult for me.

Donna is a strong, prophetic woman of God. It can be hard living with a strong, prophetic woman of God. One thing I realized was that God had sent me to Donna's to experience His love for me, but also to be trained. She lived out the love of God. In my relationship with God, I held onto guilt and bore the responsibility of my sins tightly. He wanted to remind me of His great love for me. I was struggling against wanting to earn His love and attempting to understand what He meant by grace.

One way she trained me in this was by not allowing me to help in any manner in the household. She told me I was not to work to pay them back for letting us stay with them. She and her husband, Kevin, also included us in everything they did. If they went out to eat, we went, and they paid. If they went to Dollywood, we went, and they paid for the tickets. I was also under her leadership while serving at church. She told me that she felt that God wanted her to release me from serving and that I was to take a "year off" to rest at His feet. I tend to be a "Martha" at heart, so this was extremely hard for me. I had one more thing to learn before I left Donna's home.

I always sat in the same place with the same people every Sunday. One Sunday, when I was wrestling with myself and with God, I sat somewhere else because I did not want to talk with anyone. The sermon that week was on Isaiah 53. We came to Isaiah 53:11, *which says, "He shall see the labor of His soul and be satisfied. By His knowledge, My righteous Servant shall justify many. For He shall bear their iniquities."* (NKJV) When the pastor read the scripture, I saw a vision of Jesus on the cross with a crown of thorns on His head and His blood on His face.

He turned His head to look at me and said, "I did it for you and I was satisfied to do it." He did it for me! At that moment, I finally accepted God's love and grace for me. He convicted me that if I continued to choose to remain in my guilt, I would be telling Him that what He did for me was not enough. From that moment, I would continue to ask forgiveness when I did things wrong, but once I gave it to Him, I did not grab it back. I stood forgiven.

## Kendall

After being hired by Ryan's Steakhouse, they sent me for training in Greer, SC. Penny and I were probably in the worst financial position since our marriage began. I barely had the money to drive back and forth from the apartment Ryan's had put me in. While in training, I spent time playing online gambling, which was a new thing at this point. One night after training, the other managers headed to a nightclub. We had a few days left, and the guys wanted to celebrate. I had never been to a strip club before, but that night fueled the lust within me. I was ashamed to tell Penny. Because I felt incredibly guilty, I built a major wall. At this point, I closed myself off from my wife.

## Penny

During my time with Donna, we spent time praying, worshiping, having fun, and just talking. One conversation stands out in my mind because we were talking about our husbands. We talked about the complete security we had in knowing how much our husbands loved us. I had never been jealous because I knew with absolute certainty that Kendall loved me just the way I was.

Before we moved to our new home, I went to Georgia to see Ginger. She gave me a scripture that she felt God wanted me to have before our move. Exodus 23:20 says, *"I am going to send an angel in front of you, to guard you on the way and to bring you to the place that I have prepared. Little by little I will drive them [your enemies] out from before you, until you have increased and you possess the land."* (NRSV) The word about the thorny path had given me a warning, but it also gave hope. God would eventually settle us, but it would not be quick. It would happen little by little. I would need all the hope I could get because that thorny path was going to be exceedingly long.

## Kendall

Ryan's had assigned me to Lexington, KY. It was not until Penny and I traveled to Lexington to look for housing that I opened up and confessed what had happened. It caused such pain to admit. Frankly, it was one of the hardest things I have ever had to do. Unfortunately, it was the first in a long line of mistakes I was going to make. I believe with my whole soul that every bit of this started with what I viewed on the internet. It is like the cans on a string that people attach to your car when you get married. If you do not stop to remove them, they will always be dragging along with you your whole life.

## Penny

Kendall returned from training, and we made a trip to check out our new home. While we were traveling to Lexington to find a place to live, Kendall admitted to me what had happened at training. I was upset but thankful that Kendall had confessed it to me. I knew something had been bothering him. At this point, I was still totally secure in his love for me. I had no idea that his experiences had opened the door to a "beast" that we did not want in our family. I had thought the last year would be our lowest; however, when we arrived in Lexington, it seemed we continued to make one mistake after the other.

Because we had so many debts and no money, we had to put the moving truck and deposits on a credit card. By the end of September 1998, our debt had increased to forty-two thousand dollars. God had told us to have accountability and financial counseling, but we had not immediately sought it out once we were in Lexington. Although his confession and my forgiveness had given us a reprieve, we were soon arguing again. I was doing the study on *Financial Peace* by Dave Ramsey. I attempted to get Kendall to do it with me. I wanted to go to Consumer Credit Counseling, but Kendall did not want to do that either. Instead, he started gambling on the internet. We did not have a church, and he worked every Sunday. As my expectations grew, I started nagging. I was the epitome of the contentious and angry woman in Proverbs 21:19. I knew it was falling apart before my eyes.

I honestly did not want to get a job, but after praying about it, I picked up a newspaper and immediately found a job at a church preschool. I felt peace when I interviewed, and they hired me on the spot. Mackenzie would be able to come with me to school every day and attend preschool for free. Mackenzie and I got into a schedule, and she loved preschool and her teacher. I was able to spend time with her because both my class and her class had playtime together.

Kendall

I was pretty excited about my new placement; however, my time with the company started and ended with bad decisions on my part. My personal and spiritual life suffered the whole time I worked for the company.

Penny and I barely saw each other while we lived in Lexington, and had it not been for Mackenzie, Penny would not have had anyone to talk to at all. Even when I was home, I felt distracted. As before, I spent most of my time in front of my computer. On the internet, I could lose myself in gambling and pornography. It was my way of dealing with the stress of my job. When I was home, I did not want to think about anything other than the screen in front of me. I was not happy at work due to how understaffed we were, and I was rarely home.

I had always loved soda. At the beginning of our time in Lexington, I drank a twelve-pack of Cokes every other day. After I transitioned to no sodas, I went from two hundred and forty-eight pounds to one hundred and eighty pounds. While at work, I never had time to eat, so the only time I ate was in the evenings after we had slowed down around nine pm. I had become relatively good friends with my staff, most of whom were women. I had never really gotten much attention from women in my life, so all the attention I got at work went straight to my head. It hyper-inflated my ego.

Penny

Kendall worked long hours. He was asleep when we left for school and gone when we came home from school. When he came home from work, we were in bed. Since he worked on Sundays, I picked the church Mackenzie and I would attend. I chose it the same way I decided on our previous church. I visited, and I listened. I heard the Spirit speaking the same message as my last church. I purposely did not get close to anyone at the church I attended. I took the time to be fed the Word of God and did not serve during this time.

I had extended family and friends who lived in the Lexington area, so we had a support system built in if we needed anything. I made friends at work who loved me and loved my daughter. I loved Lexington and my time with Mackenzie there. We read books and sang songs. We went to the movies and the library. We visited with my aunts and uncles, took walks, and played on the playground, all without Kendall. We missed him. I felt in my heart that we would not be in Lexington for long, so I spent the time loving and spending time with my daughter as well as loving and spending time with my God.

I believed God must have a call on our lives because He was certainly shaking me down to just Him, teaching me to let go of myself. I trusted God had a plan, and He knew what He was doing. Romans 8:28 says, *"And we know all things work together for good to those who love God, to those who are called according to His purpose."* I knew I was in His hands, and it was the safest place for me to be.

In the middle of December, I felt God was telling me to read 2 Timothy 3:1-6 to Kendall. The scripture speaks of the last days being perilous times where men will be lovers of self and money, without self-control and lovers of pleasure rather than lovers of God. Kendall seemed convicted, and we drew closer for a time. But, as usual, it was to be short-lived.

At Christmas, I was excited about our coming to a place of reconciliation and bought him a new wedding band, as he had lost his first ring. I wrote out our vows to put in a frame. He did not even get me a present. He also did not put the ring on when we left to go to East Tennessee for Christmas with our families. We drove separately because Kendall only had a couple of days off. When I returned from East Tennessee, I found that he had taken three hundred and fifty dollars out of our account. Kendall told me the water pump had blown on the car, and he had to get it replaced. I felt in my spirit that he was lying. I actually thought he was lying to me about more than the car.

Our family, Christmas 1998

# Part Three

**Revealed *(verb)*: to make known through divine inspiration; to make something hidden or secret known** (MW)

Mark 4:21-22

*Also, He said to them, "Is a lamp brought to be put under a basket or under a bed? Is it not to be set on a lampstand? For there is nothing hidden which will not be revealed, nor has anything been kept secret but that it should come to light."* (NKJV)

# Chapter Thirteen

**Brokenhearted** *(adjective)*: **overcome with grief or despair** (MW)

Psalm 147:3

*He heals the brokenhearted and binds up their wounds.*
(NKJV)

## Penny

Soon after the beginning of the year, Kendall and I were off for a couple of days together. He told me he wanted to declare bankruptcy instead of going to financial counseling. Because of the Dave Ramsey study, I did not feel we needed to declare bankruptcy because we had made our creditors a promise to pay them back. I threatened to leave if he could not stop his spending. I had even planned where I would go if I had to leave. The next night he confessed he had not spent the money on a heat pump for the car but on another woman. He had been talking to a girl at work with the intent of destroying our marriage. He told me that he had cried out to God for help. I was utterly stunned. Spending I was familiar with; another woman had never crossed my mind.

## Kendall

I spent quite a bit of my time at work joking around and flirting with the women at work. Soon, I became involved with one of them, and it, of course, affected my relationship with Penny. I did not really know what I was feeling about our marriage, but I knew I felt guilty. I finally confessed to her what I had done and agreed to get counseling from the pastor I had never met at the church Penny had been attending.

## Penny

I am so thankful God had brought me to a place of truly knowing Him and his unconditional love before we moved to Lexington. Otherwise, I am not sure I would have made it. I ran to my Father God, and He said to me, *"I will never [under any circumstance] desert you [nor give you up nor leave you without support, nor will I in any degree leave you helpless] nor will I forsake or let you down or relax My hold on you [assuredly not]!* (Heb. 13:5 AMP) I was feeling many different things. It is hard not to be physically self-conscious when your husband turns away from you to someone else. I was furious that Mackenzie and I were not more important to him. As far as the money went, I was the one who had to deal with covering for the loss of the three hundred and fifty dollars in our budget. Mackenzie and I had to pay the cost.

I felt foolish, but we serve a merciful God. I had threatened out of anger but had not talked to God about my plan to leave. Isaiah 55:12 says, *"be led out with peace."* (NKJV) After I prayed, God did not give me peace about leaving or about bankruptcy. Instead, he led me to a counselor. Kendall agreed to go. In the first session, the counselor pointed out to us that I had just freely forgiven Kendall without any remorse on his part. He said that it was important that Kendall verbally ask for my forgiveness. Kendall asked for my forgiveness and started wearing his ring again. I had forgiven him, but I still fought against anger and depression. I did the only thing I could do; I pressed into God. We went away for the weekend for Valentine's day and had a wonderful time as a family. I am sure that the reminder of how much he loved us made him feel guilty because when we returned home, he confessed to an actual sexual encounter with the woman at work. I assumed it was just a continuation of the last confession, but it was actually a new confession. This sexual encounter had happened after our first counseling session when he asked for my forgiveness.

For our entire relationship, I had always felt secure in Kendall's love for me. Now I was insecure and felt unlovable and replaceable. I blamed myself for being too nagging and for going away to visit East Tennessee. I started picking myself a part, including the things I could not change like, the calcium deposits and the effects of the illness on my body, telling myself Kendall wanted someone more beautiful and healthier than I was. God thankfully would not let me wallow in self-pity. Instead, He reminded me that I was beautiful and precious to Him. While in church one Sunday, I heard within my heart and mind, "I am your Husband." I felt it was scripture, so I looked in my concordance for the word "husband." He led me to Isaiah 54:4-6, *"For you will forget the shame of your youth...For your Maker is your husband, the Lord of hosts is His name...For the Lord has called you like a woman forsaken and grieved in spirit, like a youthful wife when you were refused."* (NKJV) From the rest of the scripture, Isaiah 54:13-14, He showed me that He is establishing me in righteousness and that Mackenzie would have peace because the Lord would teach her. I was secure in God's love for me, and that was enough.

After his last confession, Kendall did start to change. Kendall felt convicted to sell his computer and started reading his Bible. When he was home with us, he spent time with us instead of being on his computer. For so long,

I had thought of Kendall as being guilty of greed and the love of money. God brought to my attention that I was just as guilty. I gave money too much power because I was afraid. I was constantly worried we would not have enough. I had to start confessing that the Lord is our provider (Gen. 22:14) and He will supply what we need (Phil. 4:19). We were still tithing because I was the one who paid our bills, but God told me to give above the ten percent. He even had me write it down and date it to keep myself accountable for it.

## Kendall

In April 1999, I was sent to Middlesboro, KY, to help open a new store. It was good to be working at a restaurant that had a full staff. For once, I focused on management instead of running all over the restaurant putting out fires. I was able to take the time to make sure everyone was trained correctly in their positions. I had never managed so many people before. We had 165 new employees, and we needed them all. Since our opening, we had been super busy. They fired one manager for partying with employees not long after he arrived. Luckily, I was chosen as his replacement promoted to second in command and received a pay raise and a bonus every month.

## Penny

Thankfully, our rent was quite a bit less than in Lexington. The size of the apartment was smaller too. I started praying about being able to pay off debt and about where I was to work. Unfortunately, Middlesboro was a much smaller town than Lexington and jobs were scarce. A month after our move, I found out I was pregnant, and I still did not have a job. Immediately, Kendall's stress level increased.

Kendall received a promotion in October 1999. I had already started trying to figure out where we were going to put a new baby. The apartment was tiny. A piece of furniture covered every wall of the apartment with the kitchen table and chairs and our desk in the middle of the room. Rentals were scarce in the area. So, we were considering buying a mobile home, but we would have to borrow money for a down payment. I asked God to open and close doors according to His purpose for us (Rev. 3:8). Finally, it seemed doors were opening. Our debt had hurt our credit for a year, but the issues we were concerned about were not on our updated credit report. We applied for the loan and received it. However, we soon lost peace as the amount of the loan increased, and the down payment doubled. Thankfully, the company refunded the fifteen hundred we had paid in earnest money.

Because of my stress about our debt and my fear of losing him, I went back and forth between nagging Kendall and the opposite, trying to make him happy. It was a fine line. I had to constantly redirect my heart and mind to God, especially when Kendall was with me. I continued to write in my journal and write down scriptures God was giving me. I made a list of prayers I needed to have answered and notated when God answered them. I cannot tell you that I was not also full of self-pity, insecure and depressed, or that I did not frequently cry. I thanked Him for not giving up on me, but also often asked for forgiveness. He always met me wherever I was at any moment.

I also had an overwhelming fear that something would be wrong with the baby I was carrying. I had been sick quite a bit this pregnancy, and they had no other option than to put me on antibiotics. The antibiotics that were allowed for pregnant women did not get rid of the infection. The doctor said the illness could hurt the baby more than the medicine, so she put me on a stronger antibiotic even though it could also harm the baby. Once again, God was my only hope. God met me there as well and gave me Psalm 139:13, which says, *"You formed my inward parts; You covered me in my mother's womb. I will praise you for I am fearfully and wonderfully made; marvelous are your works and that my soul knows very well."* (NKJV)

As in Lexington, Kendall's hours were long. He always worked on Sunday, so it was left to me to find a church. I found a wonderful church close by in Harrogate, TN. After visiting many churches, I chose one the same way I decided on our last church. I listened. The pastor at the church in Harrogate preached the same message as my previous church. I knew the Holy Spirit was present. Mackenzie loved her new church. She had friends, and the pastor always bent down to talk with her as we were leaving.

I had found a job at JC Penney's in the mall, and I decided to enroll Mackenzie in preschool for the fall semester at a local church. Most of the mothers of preschoolers were from the community, so they had already formed friendships, but I found three moms and one dad who had recently moved to Middlesboro for their spouse's jobs. We met to let the kids play together and talked about our children, but our relationships did not go deeper. I was thankful that both Mackenzie and I had friends. We also went back to Johnson City frequently as it was only two hours away. Because all the hospitals in the area were small, I decided to deliver the baby in Johnson City.

Another door soon opened for possible housing. A family from Mackenzie's preschool had to move due to a job transfer. They had not had any offers on their house and were getting desperate, so they had decided to transfer the loan to a different owner. The house was twenty-two hundred square feet and had a payment of four hundred and eighty dollars a month, actually cheaper than our rent for the tiny apartment. We just had to qualify to take over the loan. I immediately fell in love with the house. It had two porches, a stunning view of the mountains, and three bedrooms, with one already decorated as a nursery. We agreed to rent until the loan went through, so we were moved in by the beginning of November.

Our family, Christmas 1999

I had delivered Mackenzie a week early, so my obstetrician wanted me to be closer to the hospital before my due date. So, after Christmas, I stayed with my parents instead of returning to Kentucky with Kendall. Kendall was anxious due to his promotion, taking over the finances while I was gone, and closing on the house without me. Our tithe to the church fell between the cracks, his bonus was less than expected, and closing costs were more than expected. Kendall did not do well with stress.

# Chapter Fourteen

**Forsaken *(verb)*: to turn away from entirely** (MW)

Psalm 27:10

*When my father and mother* [or husband] *forsake me, then the Lord will take care of me.* (NKJV)

## Kendall

Working in Middlesboro was much different than working in Lexington. For one, most of the staff looked up to me. It was odd, well, from my experience anyway. I had never had women flirt with me before - not openly and in front of others, including Penny. So, all the attention went to my head. I liked it; it made me feel good about myself. For a while, I did keep myself at arm's length from my staff. Another manager had gotten fired for being involved with one of our employees. We had a policy of no fraternization. But, of course, that did not stop me from flirting back.

In late December of 1999, Penny had gone home to Johnson City, TN, to stay because it was getting closer to her due date. I had stayed in Pineville to work until the baby was born. I received a call from Penny on January 12th that she was in labor. I told my General Manager but did not go immediately. Penny called again and was shocked that I had not had a chance to leave yet. I headed to Johnson City as fast as I could. I arrived at the hospital, and twenty minutes later, Kaitlin was born.

## Penny

Kaitlin Quinn Cochran was born four hours after I left my physician's office. Kendall was working in Kentucky, so I called him before leaving the doctor's office to let him know to hurry. I was alone in the hospital room, wondering if anyone would make it in time. By the time Kendall arrived, the doctor, the nurses, his mother, and my sister were all in the room. But he got there in time to see Kaitlin born.

While I was still in the hospital with Kaitlin, Kendall decided to look at new cars. I was against this and told him so. Closing costs and lack of a good bonus had hurt our finances. When Kendall picked Kaitlin and me up at the hospital, he came in a new Altima. I was shocked and upset. I knew we could not handle the payments. It hurt me to think that the main thing on his mind while I was in the hospital was buying a new car. I planned to stay in Johnson City until Kaitlin's first appointment with the pediatrician, so I did not immediately head back to Kentucky with Kendall. Even though I was so thankful for Kaitlin and joyous that she was finally here, Kendall's behavior unsettled me.

Our family after Kaitlin's birth, January 2000

## Kendall

While in Johnson City, I spent half my time at the hospital and half my time at the Nissan Dealership looking to buy a new Altima. I only had three days off from work, so I headed back to Pineville with the new car. When I arrived back at work the next day, everyone gave me hugs and congratulations about the new baby. When one of my servers, Lauren*, asked me why I did not hug her, I just shrugged my shoulders. But that got me thinking, "What is she thinking?" She had always been friendly, but I had never thought twice about it. I started talking to her more, which led to flirting, which I figured was nothing. (*name changed)

## Penny

After we returned to Kentucky at the end of January, Kendall was very attentive. I had missed him so much during my time away, so I returned home with a determination to be everything I thought he needed me to be. In the back of my mind, I believed our problems were my fault and that if I tried to be a better wife, it would fix the problems. I slept downstairs with Kaitlin so she would not wake Kendall up. I tried to make sure the house was clean and his dress shirts were ironed and pressed - all with a newborn and a three-year-old. I was exhausted.

I started tithing again, but we were extremely behind on our bills. Because Kendall worked at Ryan's, we were able to eat daily for free. That took care of at least one meal for each day. Because Kendall worked long hours, we could at least see him once a day when we ate at the restaurant. I tried to get us back on target with our finances and prayed that God would give us wisdom, help us to cover new payments, and forgive our disobedience.

Keeping busy was easy but spending time with God was difficult with two children. However, I continued to make time with God a priority. God showed me that I was secure in His love for me, but now I had started to try to earn Kendall's love. Despite the busyness, I kept God before me. Mackenzie and I praised together at home and in the car. I prayed the scriptures I had written down. I read my Bible. I cried out to God about Kendall's temptation to spend. But by February, he had charged an additional twenty-four hundred dollars in four months, not counting the new car.

I had been asking the Lord to speak to me. I needed to hear His voice. At the beginning of March, the words "Peace like a River" came to mind. My first thoughts were, "but a river isn't peaceful." The Lord then gave me the word "sanctuary" and led me to Ezekiel 47:12, which says, *Along the bank of the river, on this side and that, will grow all kinds of trees used for food; their leaves will not wither, and their fruit will not fail. They will bear fruit every month because their water flows from the sanctuary. Their fruit will be for food, and their leaves for medicine."* (NKJV) I determined to stay in His sanctuary. I wanted my fruit to be healing. However, the river was about to get rough. I am not sure I would have made it had I not kept my eyes on Jesus.

The second week in March, Kaitlin was diagnosed with Respiratory Syncytial Virus (RSV). They did not put her in the hospital but sent me home instead with a nebulizer. She would have to be fed every two hours with nebulizer treatments between day feedings. She had to sleep in her car seat to keep her head elevated. Mackenzie had an upper respiratory infection and, soon after that, caught a stomach virus.

The girls and I were going back and forth to doctors, and we were running out of money for co-pays and medicine. After an appointment with Kaitlin's physician, I realized that I needed to pick up some prescriptions and had no money to pay for them. I cried out to God to take care of the need. In the mail that same day, I received a check from my friend, Karen, with just enough money to cover the medicine. God knew my need before I even knew it. Around the same time, God told me to give a certain amount of money to a friend who had a greater need. I did not have money to go grocery shopping, much less send someone money. I told Him that I would give them the money if He gave me the money. The next day another friend sent a two-hundred-dollar check in the mail to us. I forwarded the money immediately to my friend who had the need. It was God's money, not mine.

My time with God fell by the wayside, and I had no time for Kendall amid all the chaos. I could tell he was not happy, but I had nothing left to give. I felt a wall go up between us. He found other things to do when he was off. He stopped showing concern for us and made me start driving the old car while he took the new car. He strongly encouraged me to go to Johnson City for a visit at the end of the month. He had training scheduled in South Carolina, so he would not be home anyway. So, the girls and I headed back to Tennessee. I needed a break from him and felt I needed a rest after an exceedingly difficult month. It was a mistake.

## Kendall

One night, Lauren asked me for a hug while I was taking stock and ordering. That changed everything. I did not consider anything we were doing a risk to my job because she was getting ready to leave to go to management training in South Carolina. By my thinking, when she left, the fraternization rule would not apply. I went to visit her twice while she was in South Carolina. I told Penny that I had to go to training and she believed me. It put a wall up between Penny and me like things of this nature always will. I was guilty. I was going to have to confess to my wife that I had committed adultery.

Penny

Kendall was still distant, and when I returned home, he told me he had to go back for another training. When he returned from the training, he confessed that he had had an affair with one of his past employees. The woman had received a job as a manager with Ryan's and was in training in South Carolina. She was involved with someone else and was already pregnant with the other man's child when the affair started. He said he had done everything he could to make me leave. He told me he had feelings for her, but she did not want a relationship with him.

Since we moved to Middlesboro, there had always been waitresses who openly flirted with Kendall in front of me. I had even received calls at JC Penney's from someone telling me he was unfaithful. I knew this woman. She talked with Mackenzie and me when we came to the restaurant. She had admired Kaitlin when I brought her to the restaurant the first time. When he told me, it felt like something had died within me. He admitted to an affair, not just a sexual encounter. He wanted to be with her, not me. My first reaction was to run, but I felt God was telling me to stay. I did not want to stay. I cried out to God to lead me and give me wisdom. He once again led me to godly counselors. Before, I had always kept the things Kendall had done between God and me to protect

112

him. I did not want to shield him any longer. I met with my pastor and his wife, reached out to godly friends, called the man who had married us, and I called Kendall's parents. I could not bear to tell my parents yet.

Kaitlin's baby dedication would take place at church on the following Sunday. Kendall was already off for the occasion, and his parents came soon after I called them. The church surprised me with a baby shower as well. It was not easy to smile and receive from those who loved me. All I was feeling was grief and rejection. Kendall was telling me that he loved me and that he did not want to lose me. However, he had just said that he had wanted to be with her, so it was hard to believe him.

## Kendall

Penny asked me to drive to Florence, Kentucky, and talk to Dan, an old youth minister of mine, one of the men who had officiated our marriage. I admitted everything that had happened. One thing was for sure; I was not following God's plan for my life.

Sunday Morning before Kaitlin's dedication.
Mackenzie age 3 and Kaitlin age 3 months

# Chapter Fifteen

**Sanctuary *(noun)*: a consecrated place; a place of refuge and protection** (MW)

Psalm 20:2

*May He send you help from the sanctuary [His dwelling place] and support and strengthen you from Zion.* (AMP)

Penny

After hearing counsel from several godly people on what I could do, I made Kendall a list of things to do for me to stay. Since there were no mental health counselors in the area, he needed to meet with our pastor weekly. He had to have HIV and STD testing and cancel the internet. I asked him to sit down and do the finances with me each week. I had a close relationship with his boss, and he had gone through something similar with his ex-wife. He was going to try to get Kendall off work on at least two Sundays a month. I told Kendall that he needed to go to church with me.

I met with my pastor and his wife weekly. I was struggling with grief and rejection. I did not want an intimate relationship with Kendall, but he would shut down on me and make life difficult. I reacted the same way I always did. I tried to keep him happy and would give in. My thoughts were crushing me. I knew how beautiful the other woman was; I knew her. I felt ugly, flawed, and inadequate, but God reminded me who I was in Him and how He sees me. I prayed that God would help me to stay in His sanctuary. I now understood why God had put the words "Peace like a River" in my heart. My life, mind, and emotions were full of chaos, but He alone would be my place of peace even in the raging.

Isaiah 54:6-8

*For the Lord has called you like a woman forsaken and grieved in spirit; like a youthful wife when you were refused, says your God. For a mere moment I have forsaken you, but with great mercies I will gather you. With a little wrath I hid My face from you for a moment; but with everlasting kindness I will have mercy on you, says the Lord, your Redeemer.* (NKJV)

Those first couple of months after his confession, I was utterly overwhelmed. Daily I had tremors, headaches, nausea, IBS attacks, and I could not eat. When Kaitlin first cried in the morning, it took all I had within me to get up to get her. It was a constant battle to be a good mother. I often failed and had to ask forgiveness from God and Mackenzie. Mackenzie was also struggling. She had more tantrums and disobedience, and I often did not deal with it well. While I nursed her sister, she sat on the armrest next to me with her arm around my neck. I prayed that God would put them in a bubble so that the tension would not touch them. Before bed each night, I prayed over my girls, speaking scriptures to them. I had praise time with them during the day. I had found small musical instruments for Mackenzie to play while we sang. We sang praise songs in the car. They were the only reason I got up in the morning.

Kendall did sit down to do the finances with me, but I found some things that I did not understand in the process. He lied to me at first when I asked him about the money that had come out of our account. Kendall had spent money on hotel rooms and flowers for her from a florist in South Carolina. He had bought her a calling card so she could call him at work. Before the affair, she had told Kendall, she was pregnant. Soon the father of her baby found out about the affair, and he was making threats to Kendall. The intimidation at least scared him into waking up a little.

We prayed together for the first time in a long time. The Lord gave me Isaiah 55:13, which says, *"Instead of the thorn bush the cypress tree will grow, and instead of the nettle the myrtle tree will grow; and it will be a memorial to the Lord, for an everlasting sign [of His mercy] which will not be cut off."* (AMP) It gave me hope. It gave me hope when Kendall told me the Lord had given him a word as well. Ezekiel 36:26 says, *"I will give you a new heart and put a new spirit within you; I will take the heart of stone out of your flesh and give you a heart of flesh."* (NKJV)

However, time went forward with not much change. The joy of the Lord became my only source of strength. I could rest in His sanctuary, but I did not see much difference when I looked at Kendall in the natural. Initially, Kendall had agreed to do everything on the list. However, saying you will do anything and doing them are two different things. He put off going for HIV and STD testing because he said it would cost too much money. He did initially meet with our pastor but then put off making return appointments. Most Sundays, he would not even get up for church when he was off. He sat down to do the finances with me, but we argued the entire time. He told me he had canceled the internet, but I did not realize he had not canceled because I was never on the computer. Once his fear left, he stopped wanting to pray with me.

One Sunday, I woke up with a spirit of heaviness weighing me down. I was panicked over losing my idea of a family and my house with a porch facing the mountains. I did not have peace about leaving, but something was whispering in my ear that I was a fool for staying. That morning, I met with my pastor and his wife. When I told them what I was feeling, he said, "So stay." So simple, yet so complicated. As they prayed with me, the spirit of heaviness left me, and I was back to dwelling in His sanctuary in peace. I felt the enemy constantly trying to weigh me down. It was hard to pray some days, but I knew the only way I would make it was through Him. I pushed through.

I would go from fear to faith again, sometimes within the same day, sometimes within the same hour. In my relationship with Kendall, it seemed the distance began to stretch even farther between us. But with God, again and again, I walked into His presence discouraged and depressed, and He put me back on my feet. I pulled closer to God but felt myself guarding my heart against Kendall. I never knew what I was going to get with him. One day he would be kind, and the next, he was disrespectful and belittled me in front of Mackenzie. Sometimes it felt as if I would never be whole again, that the brokenness in my heart and the brokenness in my body would never heal. I now felt as if I had entered a waiting game. I felt God saying to me, *"Wait for and confidently expect the Lord; be strong and let your heart take courage."* (Ps. 27:14 AMP)

Throughout this time, we also received continued counsel from Dan and also from Kendall's dad. They were blunt with Kendall. Dan even gave both of us homework. Kendall was sorrowful for his actions in front of them, but he did not have any follow-through. He continued to use the charge cards, would not get rid of the internet, would not attend church, and continued to lie to me. In church one Sunday, I felt my heart racing and was having trouble breathing. I went to the restroom and leaned against the stall. I heard God speak to me, *"And after having done everything, to stand. Stand firm then."* (Eph. 6:13-14 NKJV) I knew it was part of two passages from Ephesians, but it was also God's voice, and it calmed me and gave me courage.

In September, Kendall said he wanted to claim bankruptcy. This time God gave me peace. Kendall wanted to go back to Lexington to file so it would not appear in the local paper. At the appointment, Kendall was adamant about wanting to give up our home in bankruptcy. The lawyer told us it was not required because we had to have somewhere to live. Kendall was insistent. The lawyer told us we could still probably live in the house mortgage-free for 6-8 months before the bank took it to auction. His decision to give up the house took me completely off guard.

## Kendall

That fall, Penny was rear-ended in the Altima, and we had received a check for damages. I decided to keep it for myself; instead of fixing the car. I was giving it up in bankruptcy anyway. I knew that I could use it to relocate back to Middlesboro. I told myself it was so that I did not have to drive so far to get back and forth to work. But I had also heard that Middlesboro was getting cable internet. Unfortunately, we were also losing the Altima in the bankruptcy, so I bought a worn-out old car to drive to work.

## Penny

As we traveled back home after meeting with the lawyer, I silently talked to God about where we would live and what we were going to do. God spoke to my heart at that moment that my concern was to only be for the three of us. He would deal with Kendall. I felt God was telling me to leave with the girls. That night I stood on the porch of my house to say goodbye to my home. The house was His now, and so was Kendall. My dwelling place was with God.

Our house in Pineville

# Chapter Sixteen

**Clay** *(noun)*: **mud; the body distinguished from the spirit; fundamental nature** (MW)

Psalm 40:2

*He also brought me up out of a horrible pit. Out of the miry clay, and set my feet upon a rock, and established my steps.* (NKJV)

Penny

In May, I had finally told my dad about the affair but had not talked with him further about it since then. So, when I asked him to come and get us in October, I am sure he was surprised. My dad came to Pineville to collect the girls and me and load up a few possessions to take with us. I was completely overwhelmed. I was having difficulty sleeping. I was having panic attacks and also having trouble making decisions, especially about what to do next. I did apply for some social work jobs. I even had some interviews. I asked God to open doors that needed to open and close doors that needed to be closed. It seemed as if every door was slamming in my face.

Mackenzie was confused about what was happening and did not understand why we were not going back home. She had tantrums every day, and I was not dealing with them well. Mackenzie missed her daddy, her school, her friends, and her church. I felt inadequate, and that was most evident in my parenting. To my parents and my sister, I am sure it seemed that I was having a tantrum as well. I guess I was. Sometimes it feels good to rage a little. However, it did not help Mackenzie or Kaitlin. I am so thankful for my parents. I had put them in a challenging position, but they were there for all of us. They were good parents to my children at a time when I was not.

Mackenzie desperately wanted to take dance lessons, and thankfully, her grandparents were willing to pay for the classes. After she started dancing, her tantrums decreased. Like her nana, she thrived on making new friends. I also met some new friends and reconnected with an old friend from Campus House. Mackenzie missed school most of all. We had moved back to Johnson City after the fall semester had already started so, our friends at dance class were the ones who recommended putting her on several preschools' waiting lists. Surprisingly, Mackenzie received an opening in a church preschool in November. My parents had started a savings account for her when she was born, so that I could use that money for preschool. Kendall had already rented a house in Middlesboro. I had finally realized that he wanted to be back in Middlesboro because he wanted faster internet. So, he gave up our home for the internet.

Getting ready for dance class

## Kendall

After staying at this rental house and still having issues with paying bills, I came to a stark realization. If I had stayed at our home in Pineville and not moved to Middlesboro, I could have saved thirty-eight hundred dollars. But, instead, I was paying more for the rental than I had for our house payment. I was sick to my stomach for quite a while about this. Besides that, the cable internet never made it to Middlesboro while I was living there.

## Penny

I started seeing a Christian counselor and spent much of the week looking forward to seeing her again. My family and friends loved me, but it was hard to talk to them and then deal with their emotions as well as my own. Something small like a word from my mother-in-law or Mackenzie having a tantrum could send me back into depression or an anxiety attack. My counselor taught me ways to calm myself down in an anxiety attack with breathing. She told me to tell myself that it was just fear, to diminish it in my head and heart. I constantly said to myself, "This is just fear, God did not give me a spirit of fear or timidity or cowardice." (2 Tim 1:7 AMP)

The separation had shaken our world, but He held us in His hands. In my study, God gave me Ezekiel 36:35-36, which says, "*So they will say, 'This land that was desolate has become like the garden of Eden; and the wasted, desolate, and ruined cities are now fortified and inhabited.' Then, the nations which are left all around you shall know that I, the Lord, have rebuilt the ruined places and planted what was desolate. I, the Lord, have spoken it and I will do it.*" (NKJV) As always, His word to me gave me hope.

I tried my best to stay as close to the Lord as possible, but Satan knows our weaknesses. If you notice, I said I was trying my best. Mama said when I learned to talk, I would say, "I do it myself." Even though I finally understood grace and surrender, my nature was to work it out for myself. I spent quite a bit of time in my head. I would go through conversations and actions again and again in my head after they had happened. When I became stressed, my body would fight against me with migraines, IBS, sleeplessness. As I have said, my biggest sin was pride, wanting others to be pleased with me.

It was a day-by-day, moment-by-moment walk. It was difficult for me to stay in that sanctuary. If I could literally hide in the cleft of a rock with my two children, I would have. But, unfortunately, that was not possible. I had to contend with people, circumstances, and my own and everyone else's response to those circumstances. I constantly worried about how those people and those circumstances were affecting my children. I was having a lot of bad days. I continued to pray for Kendall, and I

124

asked God to restore our family. The girls and I continued our praise time in the basement of my parent's house, and I used the sunroom late at night to do my Bible study. It was a continuous process of walking out what God was telling me.

As the year 2000 was winding down, Kendall called to tell me that the woman he had had an affair with would be moving back to the Middlesboro store. Kendall said he had talked with the Regional Manager but that he would not change his mind. Kendall was sure this was a "test," and that he could work with her and it would not affect him. I gave him a choice. He needed to ask for a transfer. If his manager was unwilling to move him, he should quit. I told him he could choose them or us. He was not happy.

Kendall decided to meet with his managers again. Even if it meant he received a demotion or had to leave his job, he was willing to put our marriage first. His manager gave him a transfer to a store within the Tri-Cities region close to us. Kendall was not supposed to receive the transfer until February, and Lauren would be arriving back in Middlesboro in mid-January. Kendall kept saying he could handle it. I told him I could not, so I prayed. Without Kendall asking for a prompt transfer, the Lord worked it out for him to leave the week before she arrived.

Even though my mom wanted me to go back to my home church, I decided to return to the church that Kendall and I had attended after moving to Johnson City from Nashville. I knew I would be unable to hide at my home church. I would not have been able to go unnoticed there. I did not want to let anyone know what was happening in my family. I always tried to get in and out of the church without talking to anyone. I once again had a spirit of heaviness that I was having trouble shaking. It took everything I had to get up and get the girls ready for church, but I continued to do it.

One Sunday, I asked my pastor to pray for me. I had not talked with him about what was happening in my family or asked for his counsel. He did not even ask what I needed him to pray for that day. When he prayed, he spoke against a spirit of heaviness and against spirits who would try to destroy my family. As always, as I concentrated on Jesus and His love and grace, peace washed over me. It would be a long time before I would stay in that peace. Most days, I took my eyes off Jesus and looked only at my failures and what others thought. God continued to remind me that I could do nothing in myself. I would never be enough, but He is always more than enough.

Isaiah 30:18,21

*And therefore, the Lord [earnestly] waits [expecting, looking, and longing] to be gracious to you; and therefore, He lifts Himself up, that He may have mercy on you and show lovingkindness to you. For the Lord is a God of justice. Blessed (happy, fortunate, to be envied) are all those who [earnestly] wait for Him who expect and look and long for Him [for His victory, His favor, His love, His peace, His joy, and His matchless unbroken companionship]! And your ears will hear a word behind you, saying, This is the way; walk in it, when you turn to the right hand and when you turn to the left.* (AMPC)

# Chapter Seventeen

**Grace *(noun)*: unmerited divine favor and assistance given for spiritual renewal** (MW)

Jeremiah 29:13-14

*Then [with deep longing] you will seek Me and require Me [as a vital necessity] and [you will] find Me when you search for Me with all your heart. I will be found by you, says the Lord, and I will restore your fortunes and I will [free you and] gather you...from all the places where I have driven you, says the Lord, and I will bring you back to the place from where I sent you into exile.* (AMP)

Penny

During my walk with the Lord, I had gone from thinking that my illness was "just a cross I had to bear," to believing I would be healed, to struggling with God as to why He did not restore me to complete health. I was still dealing with frequent infections in my calcium deposits, and I was frequently on antibiotics. One night during praise time with the girls, I heard God speak into my heart, 2 Corinthians 12:9. It says, *"And He said to me, 'My grace is sufficient for you, for My strength is made perfect in weakness.'"* (NKJV) I had read the scripture many times before. I had heard sermons about why the scripture was about healing and other sermons about why it was not about healing. They had only led to confusion. However, when God speaks, it does not matter what others have said about it. I realized it also did not matter if it was about healing or living with my illness; it still applied. God was teaching me different aspects of His grace. By His grace. I stood forgiven. Only by His grace could I do what He needed me to do, and by His grace alone could I continue walking in my weakness.

As well as reminding me about His grace, God also put on my heart to research calcium deposits and their treatment in people with juvenile dermatomyositis. I discovered that surgery was the only known treatment that worked, but there was still a fifty percent chance of the deposits would return after surgery. So, I consulted a plastic surgeon to discuss the removal of the deposits on three sites on the surface of my skin that were breaking open and becoming infected most frequently. I prayed, and God gave me the peace I needed to have the surgeries. We had insurance, and my parents agreed with my decision and would be there to help me with the girls.

Mackenzie and Kaitlin with Nana

I had two separate surgeries: one on my right arm and knee and one on my left arm. After the surgery on my left arm, the plastic surgeon told me the surgery was complicated as I had calcium deposits wrapped around veins and nerves. He had to cut a vein and sew it back together. Thankfully, I would never have to deal with an open wound or infection in those sites again. I had also asked him about removing a large calcium deposit in my abdomen. But, because the other surgeries were so challenging, he said he would prefer not to do any more surgeries on me.

After the surgeries and healing were over, I once again began looking for a social work position. I sent my resume to organizations hiring for full-time positions but did not receive a call to interview with any of them. So, I started applying for part-time jobs. I finally received an interview at a local ministry to those in poverty and was hired at the interview. I only worked half days, so I placed Kaitlin in a Mother's Day program at a local church. Mackenzie had started kindergarten in the summer at a year-round public school, so my parents were relieved of having child-care duty.

It was the first social work job I had worked in five years, but I quickly got back into the swing of dealing with clients. As is usual with most social work positions, I needed quite a bit more time than my scheduled hours to do my job effectively. It was highly stressful. However, I like to do a job well, so leaving work in time to get Kaitlin when the Mother's Day Out ended for the day was just as stressful.

God's grace was definitely with me during this time concerning Kendall as well. When Kendall returned to the Tri-Cities, I convinced him to see a Christian counselor and a psychiatrist at the Christian Counseling Center. He was not consistent and missed appointments. Spending time with Kendall was like a roller coaster. You never knew what you were going to get when you were with him. Sometimes we had fun as a family. Other times, we argued. We argued about my surgery because he was

129

afraid it would cost too much. We argued when he missed appointments. We argued when he wanted to spend money he did not have. He wanted us to live with him, but I did not have peace about leaving my parent's home. The psychiatrist put Kendall on an antidepressant, but it seemed to make him worse. There was more lying and more spending money on charge cards. He made excuses for giving me less money and for not coming by as often. Kendall needed to give up his credit cards and the internet. Instead, he bought a new computer.

Finally, the counselor shared with him that he suspected Bipolar Disorder. The psychiatrist put him on a series of three medicines, an antidepressant, an antipsychotic, and lithium. He stabilized. I continued to pray scriptures God had given me over him, but most of all, I was thankful. I could finally see the light at the end of the tunnel. I loved Kendall and desired to have my family whole again. He was my home, and I wanted to return home. So, I watched Kendall for two months after he started the new medication, and in October 2001, a year after we had left, we moved back in with him.

God gave me the grace to be able to sleep on my parent's couch for a year. During that year, I dealt with surgeries, a job search, and a new job. I learned to deal with my fear, anxiety, and depression with the help of a wise counselor. I heard God's voice telling me scriptures I needed to pray, sins I needed to confess, people I needed to confess my sins to, and people I needed to talk to about Jesus. It was a painful year. Putting aside my pride and making myself vulnerable to others was the most challenging part for me, but God gave me the grace to do it.

# Chapter Eighteen

**My Keeper *(noun)*: one who keeps; protector; guardian** (MW)

Psalm 121:1-2,5-6

*A Song of Ascents "for the road"*

*I will lift up my eyes to the hills-*
*From whence comes my help?*
*My help comes from the Lord*
*who made heaven and earth.*

*The Lord is your keeper;*
*The Lord is your shade at your right hand.*
*The sun shall not strike you by day,*
*Nor the moon by night.* (NKJV)

## Penny

As I am looking back, it is incredible that my children turned out so well. Once we moved back with Kendall, I had returned once again to my old enemy, fear. I was fearful of dealing with people, afraid of confrontation, and afraid of rejection. I had a fear of failure, a fear of getting sick again, and most of all, a fear of Kendall going back to the way he had been. I started having anxiety attacks again and dreaded going to work to deal with clients. I struggled to get everything done, and I was hateful and impatient with my children. Thankfully, I believed that my children would be taught by the Lord. He was the one who would give them peace (Is. 54:13 NKJV). I was dependent on it.

I am also thankful that I knew the way back because I had been down this road before. Sometimes it is simply hard to turn it around. It is easier to sit in front of the TV, or, in my case, behind the pages of a book, than it is to spend time reading the Bible. The new apartment was small, and our bedroom was in the living room, so I had put aside my time with God. With the anxiety attacks returning, I knew I had to change. I began spending time with God in the evenings after the kids were in bed. But as I prayed, I felt a block, as if I could not get through to Him. I asked Him to show me what was wrong. I needed to hear His voice. He opened my eyes and showed me that I had made a commitment to give above my tithe. I had even written it down and dated it. I saw that I still had four hundred dollars that I needed to give, but because of my fear, fear that if I gave it, we would not have enough for other things we needed, I had not kept my promise.

It is funny how easily we forget. God is the one who supplies all our needs. He pointed out to me that I had the four hundred dollars in my savings account. I needed to let go of the money and hold on to Him instead. When I wrote the check, the Holy Spirit filled me with joy and freedom. Since I had moved back in with Kendall, I had been bracing myself for something terrible to happen, but God wanted me to let go of my fear and be obedient, trusting that He would keep me.

Kendall had agreed with me that after Christmas, I could leave the social services agency to take a job working with babies at Kaitlin's Mother's Day Out. After I started at Mother's Day Out, Kaitlin began to get sick with extremely high fevers. My mom had to take care of her because I did not have a substitute teacher for my class. While I was taking care of other people's children, my mother was taking care of mine. My mom could not handle it physically, and I also did not want her to get sick. Besides, I wanted to take care of my child. As I talked to God about the situation, He pointed out that, once again, I was still living in fear about not having enough money. I spoke with Kendall, and by the middle of March, he agreed that I could quit my job to stay home with Kaitlin.

As I spent time with God, the song, *I lift my Eyes Up*, kept running through my head. Based on Psalm 121, the song reminded me that I could trust Him and that He would keep me.

*O how I trust You, Lord*
*You are my only hope*
*You are my only prayer*
*So, I will wait for You*
*To come and rescue me*
*Come and give me life* [5]

Things were supposed to be looking up. Kendall was doing better, and we were together as a family. We had moved to a bigger place and I was able to stay home with Kaitlin. I had honored my monetary commitment to God. But still, I was unsettled. I prayed and received the distinct impression that I needed to draw even closer to Him. So, I brought several things to Him and left them at His feet.

---

[5] Brian Doerksen, "I Lift My Eyes Up" track # 7 on *Anchour Studio Sessions*, 1990, Vineyard Music.

Kendall, Mackenzie, and Kaitlin at Tweetsie Railroad, NC

First, it bothered me that Kendall still had not added me to the bank account. I knew nothing about our finances. Secondly, I had a calcium deposit on the back of my leg that became larger with each day. The fear and self-condemnation that had plagued me had to be laid before God daily as I asked Him to change my thoughts and confession to dwell on Him. I began the study, *Breaking Free* by Beth Moore. While I studied, I still had a nagging feeling that everything was not well, but I left it with Him to reveal to me what I needed to know.

I felt called to pray for Kendall and speak scriptures over Him throughout each day. I was in a fight for my marriage. I started checking the history on the computer. I discovered that Kendall was looking at pornography and matchmaking websites on the computer. After each discovery, I would talk with him about it. He would either deny it or would not respond at all. So, Kendall hid the history icon on the computer from me. God helped to find it again. I prayed harder. The girls and I spent time each day in praise and worship. Kendall had shared with me that he had never felt desperate enough to change. He was not at rock-bottom. I prayed that God would make him desperate, that He would do whatever it took to draw Kendall to Himself.

Kendall was still concerned about money and was strongly encouraging me to get a job. The amount of money he gave me for groceries was minimal, and I still was not included in our finances, so I could not look at our bank account. I started applying for jobs again. I prayed that God would close any doors he did not want open and that I would not even get an interview if He did not want me to work there. I applied for many jobs but did not get any interviews. It bothered me that I could not tithe. God reminded me of money that my parents had put in a savings account for us. I tithed 10% of that. Whenever God gave me any money, I tithed ten percent.

God laid on my heart to start a diet of fruits, vegetables, and water only, and God gave me the ability to follow through moment by moment. I still messed up at times, but I did not feel guilty. I just gave it to God and moved forward. I studied the benefits of juicing and prayed for God to send me a juicer. God sent me a two-hundred-dollar juicer for free. A calcium deposit on the back of my leg had grown to 2 inches in diameter. My doctor said something needed to be done about it soon and that I would probably need to have a skin graft. His words to me were, "It will never go away on its own." Immediately, I had a check in my spirit, "God is able."

I began to pray scriptures about healing over myself daily as well. Mark 11:23 was especially important to me, and I began to call the "mountain" of a calcium deposit to "be removed and thrown into the sea" in the name of Jesus. One Sunday at the end of July, I felt compelled to attend my dear friend Dava Lee's Sunday school class. While there, the members surrounded me, anointed me, laid hands on me, and prayed for me. Dava Lee declared that as I stood in obedience, God would wash away the deposit. She said she had a vision of water healing it.

On a Sunday morning at the beginning of August, the calcium deposit burst while I was getting dressed for church. A hard rock of calcium, soft calcium, and blood and water came pouring out of my leg simultaneously. I had to serve in the nursery that morning, so I bandaged it up and went to church. However, it continued to drain throughout the day. I had a full day planned, including having pictures made with the girls.

Nonetheless, I kept going, stopping periodically to get more bandages. The next day, however, I felt the beginnings of an infection in my body. I had a fever, and redness was going up my leg. I had not used wisdom and had not gone to have it cleaned and dressed by medical personnel. God gave me peace about going to the hospital for antibiotics, but I still did not have peace about skin graft surgery.

Picture Day with my girls, August 2002

Of course, when they saw the gaping hole in my leg, they admitted me and started me on IV antibiotics. They told me I would need skin graft surgery to cover it. Instead of arguing, I stood on the word of God and prayed. They returned the following day to tell me they had decided to try a Pulsavac ® treatment first. The Pulsavac ® would wash the site with saline and then vacuum out the infection and extra calcium. The therapist would then dress it with saline packs. My physician released me with orders to return to the physical therapist at the hospital daily. They also scheduled an appointment with a surgeon because they did not feel this treatment would heal the wound entirely. After the first visit to see the surgeon, he still thought I would need surgery, but he did not schedule it that day. Before my next visit to the surgeon, the physical therapist told me it looked great and recommended discontinuation of treatment. The surgeon and my family physician were surprised at how quickly the hole was closing on its own. Just as God had said, He healed it by water.

# Chapter Nineteen

**Hardened** *(verb)*: **to toughen, gradually acclimatize to unfavorable conditions** (MW)

Isaiah 41:10

*Fear not [there is nothing to fear] for I am with you; do not look around you in terror and be dismayed, for I am your God. I will strengthen and harden you to difficulties, yes, I will help you; yes, I will hold you up and retain you with My righteous [victorious] right hand.* (AMPC)

Penny

As September began, I started a volunteer job as the Nursery Coordinator at my church. Serving when you have a God-given grace to do it is not burdensome, but I had not stopped to ask God. I felt honored to be asked, and I just jumped in. Satan used my pride and busyness to take my full attention off God. Satan probably even set it up. I started falling away from my confession, my Bible study, and my prayer time. I started talking to others about my problems instead of taking them to God alone. I quickly became irritated with my children and inflicted guilt on Mackenzie, which caused her to be worried when she did something wrong. I allowed Satan to steal all of our peace. Realizing how I was making my children feel finally woke me up. I asked God and my children to forgive me. I realized I had to make God my priority for our family to survive.

On October 1ˢᵗ, I took a morning away to just sit with God, meditate on His word and hear His voice. I wrote, "I am sitting on a wall by a waterfall at Milligan. The sound of the water and the cool rocks at my back are soothing to my soul. I am here to hear God's voice. I want my peace and my joy back." After sitting in His presence for a while, I returned to my car. In the car, I heard the first whisper, "Peace and joy are already in you through Christ Jesus. Don't allow them to be stolen. *He* is the joy of your salvation. *He* is your peace."

I believe Satan was keeping me busy so I would not hear God's voice. I was almost too busy to see what was happening with my husband. I had been in intense prayer for him for the last year. Now, I had taken my eyes off God and almost missed the signs Kendall was sending. On October 5ᵗʰ, I wrote, "I was convicted yesterday about not spending time with Him and not praying for those He has called me to pray for. Actually, in my busyness, I have barely prayed at all. Kendall has not been having a good, few weeks. He has been impulsively spending, buying things when we are in the negative in our checking account. He's been making statements about money and referring to things as "his." He told me he would buy his own Christmas present since it was "his" money anyway. Please Lord, reveal things hidden to me and bring him out of captivity."

## Kendall

Things were not great money-wise. It was tight, and I was having a lot of stress at work. I had an area supervisor at Ryan's who blamed all the restaurant's problems on me. I was the only manager on duty and worked seven days a week from 6:30 am to 12:30 am. Spending money was my way to deal with stress. I did not see Penny or the girls at all at this point. They were asleep when I got home and sleeping when I got up to leave. As my stress increased, temptations increased. I spent much of my time at work talking to my female servers. Unfortunately, I believe that each time I became involved with another woman, the next time came easier. I once again became involved with someone at work. Sometimes I did not go home after work. However, the guilt was always the same. It pretty much steamrolled anything that used to be spiritual in my life. I avoided anything spiritual at all because it would shine a light on the darkness in my life. Finally, one day I just gathered all my stuff and left.

## Penny

Besides spending money impulsively again, Kendall did not come home from work until the early morning hours. We rarely saw him. At one point, Mackenzie asked if "Daddy was on vacation" because she had not seen him in several weeks. He always had excuses for why he had to spend or why he had to work so late. Kendall had gotten rid of the internet but decided he needed it back. Even though he was always on the computer when he was home, the computer did not show any history. Kendall's history had never been empty. On Wednesday, October 9th, we had an early appointment to see our marriage counselor. We had been meeting with the marriage counselor regularly for the last year. On Tuesday evening, I took the girls to my parents to spend the night. When I returned home, Kendall was gone. I did not hear from him until Thursday when he came by to gather some of his things and give me a letter.

In the letter, Kendall reminded me that I had told him that our marriage would be over if he ever cheated on me again. However, he said he would not pay to file for divorce, so that would be up to me. I am not sure where he was staying, but I assumed it was with the woman he was seeing. Kendall came by the house once during the next couple of weeks. Both times he was dressed up and smelling of cologne. He paced around me, threatened to take those things most important to me, and seemed to take pleasure in scaring me. It was extremely unlike Kendall. I knew something was wrong. Cindy, a good friend who was a counselor, told me that if Kendall were manic, he would come back down to depression. It reminded me of Newton's law of motion which states: "what goes up must come down."

By the end of October, he returned to stay. He was very depressed. That night he got all of the knives out of the drawer and laid them out on the table. I was afraid. I loaded up the things we needed most, and the girls and I went to my parent's home. I called his dad to let him know I was concerned. I told him I was leaving and asked him to come to be with Kendall. I needed him to try to get Kendall to get help. Kendall checked himself into a psychiatric hospital a few days later.

Back at Nana and Papaw's, November 2002

Talking to Kendall once he was at the hospital, he admitted that he had decided to take himself off his medication. He felt that he was doing better and did not need them any longer. Unfortunately, when a person suddenly goes off all his medications for Bipolar Disorder, especially ones like lithium, a person can experience a worsening of bipolar symptoms.

## Kendall

I checked myself into Woodridge Psychiatric Hospital for a week under watch due to the thoughts of suicide. While there, Penny told me she was divorcing me, which sent me into a tailspin. After being released, I moved to my older sisters' home. Her husband was leaving to serve in the Army, and they had an extra bedroom.

## Penny

Although relieved Kendall was safe in the hospital, I still had extreme grief. I did not think I could go through it again. I knew Kendall was sick. I wanted it to work, but it had been a long thorny path. I had had to deal with massive debt, pornography, bankruptcy, and other women. So, I cried out to God, and He released me to file for divorce. During this time of grief, God gave me several visions to comfort me. In my mind, I saw myself as a small child reaching up to put my small hand in Father God's much larger one. I saw Him as my father, but also my husband, my provider, my protector, my comforter, and my helper. In another, I saw myself on a path with Jesus up ahead of me. He would turn around, every once in a while, to coax me forward. I knew I was not alone.

While Kendall was in the hospital, I told him I would be filing for divorce. I wanted to let him know while he was there and could be watched and talk about it with counselors. Some people judged me for asking for a divorce, but also for asking while he was sick. But God had given me peace, so I moved forward. While he was in the hospital, I moved all of our things out of the house. By the time Kendall got out of the hospital, we were at my parent's home. When he would visit the girls, he often tried to kiss me and told me he loved me. I had been through this before - him wanting me back, saying that he had changed. It may have been an illness, but there were also some heart issues, and I was not ready to take it on again.

Kendall and Mackenzie after release from the hospital

I had been applying for Social Work positions for an entire year and had not received an interview. I had moved in with my parents at the end of October, and by mid-November, I had a full-time job. I will not lie. It was challenging being a single mom. I had quite a bit of stress at work and at home. I often slept walked – something I did in extreme stress. My counselor taught me to keep a notepad by my bed to clear my mind before sleep. I made lists until the moment I fell asleep. Kaitlin did not like daycare and chased me from the building. Mackenzie was having anxiety, tantrums, and headaches. I was depressed and wanted to bury myself in a book and go to a job where I did not have the time to think. I started eating constantly and tried not to think about why I was doing it. I started avoiding talking to God except to say, "I'm sorry." I felt like a failure as a mother, a disciple of Christ, and even a good person. When I went to church, I just cried throughout the entire service.

The depression lasted for two weeks. Ginger called one day from Georgia, where she was living. As soon as I answered, she said, "What is wrong?" Everything came pouring out to her. She prayed for me over the phone, and I physically and mentally felt the depression leave. I could move forward. Thankfully, God was with me. It seemed that Satan was doing everything to get me to give up. Both of the girls started having tantrums. They fought over everything from the moment they woke up until they fell asleep at night, and I struggled to control my temper.

There is a saying, "What doesn't kill you makes you stronger." God had been hardening me for quite some time, but I still had many lessons to learn. Through interactions at work and at home, I was learning how to deal with confrontation. I was learning to admit to being wrong without trying to excuse or justify myself. But most importantly, I was learning to be with Him, dwell in His presence, even during conflict. At work one day, a co-worker found out about my divorce. I had not talked about it. I just did my job. She asked me how I dealt with my job so well and had so much peace in the middle of a divorce. It gave me an opening to talk with her about Jesus.

In March 2003, the divorce was final. The parenting plan gave Kendall a week of vacation with the girls yearly. Kendall's lawyer asked the judge for the upcoming week. It was the most painful week of my life. On that

Wednesday, I went to church. During worship, I had a picture of Jesus holding me in His arms. Within minutes, I felt Dava Lee's arms wrapped around me in comfort. They were the arms of Jesus.

Before the sermon on that Wednesday night, I decided I needed to talk to my friend, Mary, who would be in the nursery. Unfortunately, Mary was not there that night, but Kaitlin and Mackenzie were. They had been away from me for four days, and I had not talked to them. The girls looked at me like they did not know what to do. I held them both but had to tell them that their daddy would be there to pick them up after church. Walking away from them that night was one of the hardest things I ever had to do. Kendall had not been in the church service, so I assumed he left them there for free babysitting. The week only got worse as Kendall took them to his parent's house for the rest of the week. He was off work, but he said he needed a break. Kaitlin was overwhelmed after seeing me, so she had continuous tantrums. Her grandparents did not handle it well. The song, *Hold Me, Jesus,* by Rich Mullins echoed through my heart.

*Well, sometimes my life just don't make sense at all.*
*When the mountains look so big*
*And my faith just seems so small*
*So, hold me, Jesus*
*Cause I'm shaking like a leaf*
*You have been King of my glory*
*Won't You be my Prince of Peace*[6]

---

[6] Rich Mullins, "Hold Me Jesus," track #4 on *A Liturgy, a Legacy, and a Ragamuffin Band,* 1993, Reunion Records.

We survived the week away from each other. Mackenzie came away from it more peaceful. However, Kaitlin took a while to settle down and had tantrums for a week. Kendall had struggled during the week as well, and it would be a while before he even asked to take them again, even overnight. After seeing the girls at church that week, I had moved closer to my Savior, praising Him, and reading His Word. He gave me Isaiah 61:3, which says, *"...to console those who mourn in Zion, to give them beauty for ashes, the oil of joy for mourning, the garment of praise for the spirit of heaviness; that they may be called trees of righteousness, the planting of the Lord, that He may be glorified."* (NKJV) It was a promise I would hold close to my heart. But I was still thankful to have my babies back.

# Part Four

**Restored *(verb)*: to give back; return; to renew to a former state** (MW)


Joel 1:4; 2:25-26

*What the chewing locust left; the swarming locust has eaten;*
*What the swarming locust left; the crawling locust has eaten;*
*And what the crawling locust left; the consuming locust has eaten...*
*So, I will restore to you the years that the*
*swarming locust has eaten,*
*The crawling locust,*
*The consuming locust,*
*And the chewing locust,*
*My great army which I sent among you.*
*You shall eat in plenty and be satisfied,*
*And praise the name of the Lord your God,*
*Who dealt wondrously with you;*
*And my people shall never be put to shame.* (NKJV)

# Chapter Twenty

**Joy *(noun)*: the settled assurance that God is in control of all the details of our lives, the quiet confidence that ultimately everything is going to be all right, and the determined choice to praise God in all things.**[7]

Nehemiah 8:10

*I will not sorrow for the joy of the Lord is my strength.* (NKJV)

Penny

I am so thankful that I serve God, who pursues me with his love. I have always been serious and dutiful by nature, but I now longed for joy. I need to capitalize that word with an exclamation point. Joy! It seemed that I had been so full of grief and sorrow for so long that I had trouble coming up for air. In my journaling, He put into my heart to write down the desires of my heart. In Psalm 37:4, it says, *"Delight yourself also in the Lord and He shall give you the desires of your heart."* (NKJV) I like that word too. Delight. I admit that I felt uncomfortable asking for things that were not needs, but I felt that God wanted me to write my desires down. My funds were limited. I did not make much money, but I knew my

---

[7] Kay Warren. 2012. *Choose Joy: Because Happiness Isn't Enough.* United States: Revell Books.

Father loved me and that He was a miracle-working God. So, I wrote Him a letter:

*5/2/03*

*Dear Father,*

*I feel a need to write down very specifically what my desires are. First and foremost, I hunger for You - a closer walk with You, to know Your heart and Your wisdom. I want Your heartbeat, Lord. I want to dwell where You are. It's ALL about You, Jesus. If my desires do not line up with Yours, I want Yours.*

*Secondly, I desire and long for my whole family to have a close walk with You; that my children would love and would desire to seek You on their own. Finally, I want to be a good mother who does not hinder Your plans for Mackenzie and Kaitlin.*

*I want these three things above all else. But there are some other things that I desire: some selfish, some not. So, I put them in Your hands.*

*I want to carry out the plans You have for my life, and to do everything You have destined for me to do, to stay on the path You have chosen for me, and to take as many as I can with me as I go.*

*I want to be well and my body to move as it should.*

*I want a house with a porch, a place of peace, a home with trees, and a yard with room to play and move.*

*I want Kaitlin to have a preschool where she will be cared for but also learn.*

*I want more than enough to pay my bills, buy clothing and food, but also be able to do fun things with my children.*

*I ask for joy and to be able to enjoy my children. I want my children to be taught by You and to have Your peace.* (Is. 54:13 NKJV)

Soon after the divorce, Kendall had let me know that the dealership would soon repossess my car. It was in his name alone. I did not want it repossessed from my parent's driveway, so I took it and parked it where Kendall was staying. My sister wanted a new car, so I took over her lease payments and put the insurance in my name. When the lease was up a year later, I applied for a loan; and even with the bankruptcy on my record, I obtained four percent interest for two years; and my payment was one hundred dollars less than the lease.

When God put it on my heart to give someone money above my tithe, I gave it. But God gave me so much more. In one instance, I received double the money I had given. In August 2003, my friend Sherry called to let me know she had found me a house. We went together to look at it. As soon as I drove up, I knew it was God's work. The house had a front porch, three bedrooms, and a large yard. The price was much lower than I expected, and I signed a lease that day. The house filled me with joy. The rooms were full of color and made me happy, and I felt peace residing there.

A place to call our own, August 2003

153

Because Kendall had received a new job, I signed Kaitlin up for a Christian preschool that was an all-day program. I could handle my bills alone, so Kendall just paid Kaitlin's school bill. By November, Kendall had lost his job. I asked God what to do. I only made two thousand dollars a year above the poverty level. Due to my low income, Mackenzie qualified for free lunch. Kaitlin loved her new school, but I was unsure how I would pay for it. Immediately after I asked Him, God reminded me about my mileage check. It had increased recently. I felt peace about leaving her enrolled at the preschool.

I knew God was upholding us. Every time I began to lose heart, feeling stressed or fearful, God would remind me, "I will help you. You don't have to be afraid of the future." Whenever I became negative about myself, my life, my body, He reminded me to give it to Him. He told me I was beautiful and reminded me of Isaiah 54:11-12. He was laying my foundation with precious jewels. Often, I would comfort myself in the night and picture myself being held by Jesus so I would go to sleep in peace. I could leave everything at His throne.

At Christmas, I had a tree with our family ornaments on it. God provided for the girls by sending Toys for Tots to our church. I was chose their gifts just like if I had gone to a store. The girls had received bikes for Christmas. We had terrific older neighbors, and we all sat on our porches and watched them ride their bikes. Every day, when we came home, I found little presents on my porch from my neighbors. In turn, we visited and baked them cookies. It felt wonderful to be loved and have community. James 1:17 says, "Every good and every perfect gift is from above, and comes down from the Father of lights, with whom there is no variation or shadow of turning."

(NKJV) I praised God for every gift I received, no matter how small.

Christmas 2003

As the new year came, I realized that I would get the Child Tax Credit. Because of this, I was able to buy Dollywood passes for the year, and I had money to go to the beach with my parents. I even started putting money aside for a trip to Disney World in the Fall. He was fulfilling my dream to be able to do fun things with my children. They both took dance as a gift from my parents. It was incredible to me that God does care about the little things. He had been pouring out His riches on me. As I was faithful to give into His Kingdom, He poured out His blessing on me. I wrote in my journal, "Life is good. I stand amazed especially when I look back, for how truly blessed; shaken down, and overflowing blessed we are." We had food. We had clothes. We went on vacation. We could give into His Kingdom. We danced. We sang. God had sent me Joy!

Ephesian 3:20-21

*Now to Him who is able to do exceedingly abundantly above all that we ask or think, according to the power that works in us to Him be glory in the church by Christ Jesus to all generations, forever and ever. Amen* (NKJV)

# Chapter Twenty-one

**Endurance *(noun)*: the ability to withstand hardship; to sustain prolonged stressful effort** (MW)

Hebrews 10:36-39

*For you need endurance, so that when you have done the will of God, you may receive what was promised. For yet "in a very little while, the one who is coming will come and will not delay; but my righteous one will live by faith. My soul takes no pleasure in anyone who shrinks back." But we are not among those who shrink back and so are lost, but among those who have faith and so are saved.* (NRSV)

Penny

I was joyful, but I was also tired. Being a single working mom is exhausting. However, slowly I was learning to be content in all circumstances. I was thankful I had finished my degree before I had children. I was also grateful that I was could still do fun things with the girls. I never took being able to work or even walk for granted. I knew that I could do, as it says in Philippians 4:13, *"all things through Christ who strengthens me."* (NKJV)

Even though I was not dealing with any severe health problems, I had started having migraines, muscle aches, and stiffness from the calcium deposits hardening within my muscles over time. There were some things I had never been able to do like, touching the ground, sitting on, or getting up from the middle of the floor, but my stiffness was increasing. I used some of my extra money to get a membership at a gym which improved the headaches and body aches. I was also dealing with symptoms such as depression, anxiety, IBS, and difficulty swallowing. After several tests, my doctor put me on an antidepressant with serotonin and omeprazole. He also put me on a migraine medication that had proved successful for my mom. I did not like being dependent on these drugs, but they, along with the exercise, helped tremendously.

There were also some possible changes at work on the horizon, and I felt the stress of not knowing what the future held. My job was full-time, but there was an option to have full-time with summers off. Because of the Child Tax Credit, I knew I could make it work. I was spending over eight hundred dollars a month on childcare in the summer, so I thought I might even be able to save money. I would also have more time with my children. So, I began praying for a job opening within my organization. An opportunity came open within three months. I applied for the position in May, and by July, I started the school year in a new school. It would not help for the summer of 2005, but it would for future summers.

Penny at work, Fall 2004

I was also praying about what to do about our living situation. I loved the house we were in, but my landlord had told me that if I could not buy it, she would have to put it on the market, and I would have to be out by the end of July. I had a friend come by to look at it, but he found many electrical and plumbing issues. I did not feel peace about buying it. I felt a huge loss at leaving the house and my neighbors, but God and my sister came through again. She was getting married, so instead of putting her condo on the market, she let us move in when our lease was up. The timing worked out perfectly. Since I paid her mortgage payments instead of rent, I saved another one hundred and fifty dollars per month.

I was also praying that Kaitlin would get into the free preschool at the elementary school. It was another change for her, which always caused her stress. But, on the plus side, she would stay in the same school for seven years. Also, saving four hundred dollars a month would be a blessing. Kendall had changed jobs twice since the last time he had lost a job. He was not making much money and was living in a tiny studio apartment, so child support fell by the wayside. Even without child support, I still tithed and was still able to give above the tithe when God prompted me. There were only twenty positions in the preschool, but we found out Kaitlin received one of them right before school started.

Kaitlin's first day of Preschool at Woodland Elementary

With Kendall, my feelings had changed entirely. I still loved him and wanted what was best for him, but the love had changed. It was no longer romantic. It was a love given to me by God. I had forgiven him. I was not grieving any longer. He still was not making much money, so he decided to take a job in Virginia and move to Abingdon. He started getting the girls to spend the weekend with him there. When I went out with my co-workers, they would often say, "You seem like your still married." They wanted to "teach me" how to get a date. But I was not interested in dating. I could not imagine bringing anyone new into my girls' lives. I was open to whatever God wanted to give me, but I was not seeking a new husband.

My prayers were continuously before God for my children. I prayed they would be taught by the Lord, and that great would be their peace (Is. 54:13 NKJV) because

I knew that I frequently missed it. I prayed they would have teachable, humble spirits and be able to take firm hold of instruction and not let go (Prov. 4:13 NKJV). I prayed that as they grew, they would walk with wise men and be wise, not a companion of fools (Prov. 13:20 NKJV). I prayed He would knit them together in love to godly friends and relationships, and they would come to a full assurance of understanding, to the knowledge of the mystery of God, both the Father and of Christ Jesus (Col. 2:2 NKJV). I prayed He would order their steps (Ps 37:23 NKJV), that they would love the Lord their God with their whole hearts (Deut. 6:5 NKJV), and they would hunger and thirst for righteousness and be filled (Matt. 5:6 NKJV). Finally, I prayed they would know His voice and not follow the voice of strangers (Jn. 10:4-5 NKJV).

The girls and I prayed and spoke scriptures out loud on the way to school. When they were worried about a test at school, I had them repeat, *"I can do all things through Christ who strengthens me."* (Phil. 4:13 NKJV) I reminded them they could pray in their minds and ask Jesus to help them during school. I had them repeat, He has filled me with the Spirit of God in wisdom and understanding, in knowledge and all manner of workmanship. (Ex. 35:31 NKJV). When they were afraid, I had them repeat Psalm 91. I prayed His word that they were putting into their spirits and speaking from their mouths would not depart from them (Is. 59:21).

I prayed the peace of God, which passes all understanding, would guard our hearts and minds through Christ Jesus (Phil. 4:6-7 NKJV), and His peace would reign in our home. I prayed my love for them would be patient and kind (1 Cor. 13:4 NKJV), and I would speak words of life to them (Jn. 6:63 NKJV). I prayed He would show me great and mighty things that I did not know (Jer. 33:3 NKJV) to understand their needs and personalities. Finally, I prayed as I kept His word the love of God would be perfected in me (1 Jn. 2:5 NKJV).

I knew I needed to continuously renew my mind with His word and be wholly dependent on Him. Saying scripture out loud every day put it in my heart. His word was helping me grow in the present but also building a foundation to stand on in the future. He prompted me to repent when I needed to because I knew I was a sinner saved only by God's grace. However, I also knew I could leave it at His throne and not carry it around.

# Chapter Twenty-two

**Loneliness** *(noun)*: **being cut off from others** (MW)

The loneliest moment in someone's life is when they are watching their whole world fall apart, and all they can do is stare blankly. -F. Scott Fitzgerald

## Kendall

I have been thinking about the word erotica - that is the word that started this trip. The term was first used in 1819 by King Frances about the artwork he viewed of antiquities found in Pompeii after the Mount Vesuvius volcanic eruption in 79 AD. I could compare it to my life in that like the eruption had destroyed that city, pornography destroyed my thoughts, corrupted my life, and contributed to the loss of my family. It led me to seek involvement with people who should not have had a place in my life. It ultimately led me away from the plans God had for me.

Since the divorce, I had pretty much avoided God. Who am I kidding? Before we had divorced, I was already ignoring God. But now, I finally had a reason to be angry with Him. Often when you are not doing what you are supposed to do, Satan tends to leave you alone. Why should he be worried when you are not doing anything for God's Kingdom?

After working at several restaurants, not being paid much in most, and then being fired by the one that allowed me to make a decent wage, I moved to Abingdon, VA. I moved to take a position at Sprint PCS as a customer service representative, but primarily to be close to the person I met online who lived there.

I dated several women while I lived in Abingdon, but I knew that none of the relationships would go anywhere. I honestly did not plan to be permanently attached to anyone or anything. Every relationship I had ended badly, which was quite exhausting. I constantly got reminders of what happened with my marriage and why it was my fault. With everyone I dated, I always found out I was not the only one they were seeing. However, no matter whom I was with, I was still lonely.

2005

Sprint was a low-paying job, so during this time, I continuously floated pay-day loans to get from check to check. It did not take long to realize that I would not be able to support myself or pay child support for my daughters working for Sprint. A guy at my apartment complex told me his workplace was hiring coal miners due to miners retiring. I thought, "I could do that," especially considering the amount of pay and benefits I would receive. I took a course at the University of Virginia at

Wise to obtain miner papers and accepted a job at a coal mine near Appalachia, VA.

I had never had a job like this. It was a physically demanding job, but I learned quickly, and something inside me found fulfillment as I had never had before. I was still having a hard time with money and still had considerable debt, primarily due to pay-day loans. I was constantly shopping online. My desire for stuff and technology seemed endless. I continued to dig my hole deeper by getting more into debt.

Sins are like weeds. They grow and grow, spreading into all manner of things. They have to be managed, cut, burned, and the roots killed. It seemed that no matter what I did, they always seemed to return. I had not taken the time to understand the depth of those roots or just how far, and wide those roots spread. The sins of pride, greed, and lust became entwined.

Even though I continued to have relationships with other women while in Abingdon, it was during this time that I finally started to grow up. I had never been much help to Penny. I honestly did not even know how to take care of myself. If there were any blessings to being divorced, it was that God taught me what it would be like to spend time in a desert - utterly alone, with my only alternative being to face all my issues, come to the end of myself, and trust in Him for water.

# Chapter Twenty-three

**Rejoice *(verb)*: to give joy; to make glad; the action or expression of joy** (MW)

Psalm 126;1-3,5-6

*When the Lord brought back the captivity of Zion,*
*We were like those who dream.*
*Then our mouth was filled with laughter,*
*And our tongue with singing.*
*Then they said among the nations,*
*"The Lord has done great things for them."*
*The Lord has done great things for us*
*And we are glad.*

*Those who sow in tears*
*Shall reap in joy.*
*He who continually goes forth weeping,*
*Bearing seed for sowing,*
*Shall doubtless come again with rejoicing,*
*Bringing his sheaves with him.* (NKJV)

Penny

At the beginning of each year, I ask the Lord to give me vision for the new year. I usually begin to see a pattern with scriptures that come to my attention in my reading, in the songs I hear, or a word that keeps coming to my mind. In my Bible reading, a verse will often stand out. When that happens, I stop and meditate on it and read it again and again. Sometimes He gives me insight into what

He wants me to understand. Other times I just know He wants me to remember it. So, I read it, write it down, and date it. Then, I meditate on those scriptures throughout the year, praying them and letting them sink deep into my spirit. The scriptures God gave me for 2006 were about rejoicing and blessing, I was feeling blessed already, but I was excited to see what else God would do.

In 2005 when I found out I would have to move from the house into my sister's condo, I had started praying about buying my own home. It had not yet been seven years since the bankruptcy, but I had been diligent with paying my bills, so I was hopeful. A scripture that had jumped out at me during that time was Psalm 107:29-30, which says, *"He calms the storm, so that its waves are still. Then they are glad because they are quiet; so, He guides them to their desired haven."* (NKJV) So, I gave the dream of a home of my own to God once again.

I worked at several different preschools within our organization as a social worker with low-income families. My caseload was usually thirty-two families, but as 2006 began, my caseload increased to seventy-four families. I had a forty-five-minute drive one way to areas unfamiliar to me. I was exhausted and stressed, but I felt God sustaining me. However, at an appointment with my physician, he decided that I needed an updated bone density test. The test showed that I was in osteoporosis again. He referred me to an osteoporosis specialist who gave me an injection to treat the illness. As usual, I looked up scriptures about bones, wrote them down, turned them into prayers, and said them out loud. God was still in control. I was not worried.

In May, when school was out, I decided to prequalify for a home loan. At a birthday party of one of Mackenzie's new friends, I met another mom who was a realtor. She was also a strong Christian. I told her what I had prequalified for, which was not much, asking her if she thought I could find a house with that budget. She offered to set up some showings for us, and our journey began. Finally, after looking at several homes, my realtor decided to show me a house that she and her husband owned. It was close to my parent's place on Indian Ridge and in the girls' school district.

The house on Indian Ridge, 2006

The house was a two-bedroom with a bath, but she said they could build a wall across an unused space to add a third bedroom. They had even put in new windows, doors, and carpet in the girls' rooms. They were asking a little above my prequalified amount but not by much. When I went to talk to the bank, they approved the loan. I was a little concerned about the closing costs because they could only tell me an estimated amount, and I only had a thousand dollars saved. I asked God to take care of it and left it in His hands. When I went to closing, I discovered I only owed eleven dollars! Before moving into the house, I had friends who offered to paint and even paid for the paint. I had friends who helped me update the kitchen and tear down wallpaper. I continue to be astounded by God's goodness to me to this day.

Mackenzie and Linnea on our front porch

In July, my niece, Linnea, came to live with us. Her mom, Kendall's sister, needed to travel for her job in nursing. Linnea shared Kaitlin's bedroom and started attending the girls' school. In 2006, Kaitlin was six, Linnea was eight, and Mackenzie was ten. I remember the years in that house as being so much fun. We had sleepovers and parties with their friends. They played in the snow and slid down our hill on a sled. The same hill was also a good spot for their water slide in the summer. I was able to get internet and cable for the first time, so we watched quite a bit of Disney Channel. The girls had decided to stop taking dance and instead played sports, so we spent lots of time at the gym and on the soccer field. I had a vast support system of friends: old friends, friends from church, and friends from school. We ate together, we laughed, and we took care of one another's children. The house was full of play, laughter, and friends.

Mackenzie, age 10; Linnea, age 8; and Kaitlin, age 6

The girls still saw their dad, but my friends and family were the ones who were there when I needed something. My friends moved us to the new house, my sister gave me a couch, my mama kept the girls to give me a break, and my dad insisted on mowing my lawn. I saw Kendall when he picked up the girls, but we did not have much of a relationship otherwise. In May of 2006, two co-workers at different schools asked me about my marital situation on separate occasions. These co-workers shared their testimonies of restored marriages with me - both after similar situations as mine. Both stated they wanted to pray for my relationship with Kendall. At the time, I was not even willing to be thankful for their prayers. I asked them to please pray for Kendall, to even pray for me, but not to pray for "us."

That summer, Kendall began dating a woman from Abingdon who had a son. Kendall decided he wanted the girls to meet them. Kaitlin did not remember us being together as a couple, so for her, it was just meeting new friends. But for Mackenzie, it was devastating. After one outing, she broke down, telling me it was hard to watch her dad spend time with another family like it was his own. The next time Kendall came for a visit, I told him he needed to talk with her. As she sobbed in his arms, he was at a complete loss. He broke up with the woman soon after.

By the end of 2006, Kendall had decided to move back to Johnson City. He was still working as a coal miner in Virginia, but the drive from his work to Johnson City was the same distance as the mine to Abingdon. So, he moved in with a friend he had met when he worked as a restaurant manager and began spending considerably more time with the girls.

# Chapter Twenty-four

**Change *(verb)*: to give a different course or direction to; to undergo a modification** (MW)

The world as we have created it is a process of our thinking. It cannot be changed without changing our thinking. -Albert Einstein

## Kendall

After four years on my own, I finally got to a point where I was honest with myself. I was unhappy - completely miserable and tired of thinking only about myself. I had been this way for a long time. I had been spending my time with people I should not be associated with and making terrible decisions. Yet, God still had plans for me. I could finally see them and could not ignore them any longer.

Penny and the girls were in Johnson City, and it was not easy to keep driving back and forth from Abingdon when I needed to see my family. Because married or not, Penny was still my family. And in the back of my mind, I had always hoped that if I ever came to my senses, I would be able to fix and heal the chasm I had created between us.

I had finally decided that there was no reason for me to live in Abingdon. A friend of mine in Johnson City had a room available to rent, so I moved in with him. Until this time, I had not been faithful in helping Penny financially. The room was pretty cheap, a lot cheaper than living in Abingdon. It enabled me to start giving Penny more financial help. To be honest, my child support payments had been sporadic at best. I constantly made terrible financial decisions. After moving back to Johnson City, I finally started taking care of my financial obligations.

I enjoyed being closer to the girls - to spend time with them and pick them up from school. I decided to talk to Penny and ask her if I could move into the basement and pay her rent to live there. Reluctantly, she agreed. After staying there just a short time, she noticed I was different. I was constantly doing things to help her that she did not ask me to do. I took over mowing the yard. I took out the trash. I stayed with the girls so she could have some time for herself. All of the things she would have had to ask me to do in the past. She knew this was not like me.

Kendall and Kaitlin, Christmas 2006

# Chapter Twenty-five

**Lovingkindness***(noun)*: **tender and benevolent affection** (MW)

Isaiah 30:18, 19b, 21

*And therefore, the Lord [earnestly] waits [expecting, looking, and longing) to be gracious to you; and therefore, He lifts Himself up, that He may have mercy on you and show lovingkindness to you. For the Lord is a God of justice. Blessed (happy, fortunate, to be envied) are all those who [earnestly] wait for Him, who expect and look and long for Him [for His victory, His favor, His love, His peace, His joy, and His matchless, unbroken companionship] ...You shall weep no more. He will be very gracious to you at the sound of your cry; when He hears it, He will answer you...And your ears will hear a word behind you, saying, This is the way; walk in it.* (AMPC)

Penny

In January 2007, I asked God to give me a vision for my year with Him. He gave me several scriptures: Old and New Testaments. At first, I thought most of the scriptures had to do with Linnea, but as I continued to say them and meditate over them, the Lord began to reveal more. With the revelation, my first thought was, "You have got to be kidding!" As well as several others, He impressed upon me Isaiah 54:2,4, which says, *"Enlarge the place of your tent, and let them stretch out the curtains of your dwellings; do not spare; lengthen your cords, strengthen your stakes. For you will expand to the right and to the left...For you will forget the shame of your youth and will*

175

*not remember the reproach of your widowhood anymore."* (NKJV) He also gave me Isaiah 58:12, which says, *"Your ancient ruins shall be rebuilt; you shall raise up the foundations of many generations; you shall be called the repairer of the breach, the restorer of streets to live in."* (NRSV)

As I poured the word of God into my heart, my heart began to change toward Kendall as well. By the Spring of 2007, Kendall had asked if he could move into my basement. He wanted to give me the money he was spending on rent. I agreed. I could use the money, and I could watch how he parented. I could see a change in Kendall; maybe it was just having a piece of his family again, but it was nice. He was more peaceful, and he went out of his way to provide for our family. He started attending and serving in church again. He acknowledged how much he had hurt me and began trying to make amends. Even the little things meant so much to me.

In June, the girls and I had scheduled a trip to the beach with my parents. I was at my parent's house the week before we left on our trip, helping them pack. Mid-sentence, my mom started talking incoherently. I immediately called her neurologist, who told us to get her to the hospital as quickly as possible. Since her physical abilities had not changed, we loaded her into the car instead of waiting on an ambulance. She had had a stroke. Thankfully, the stroke had only affected the left hemisphere of her brain, so her physical abilities were the same as before. She could still talk. However, she could not put a sentence together that made sense. She also could no longer read or write. It was hard to watch. My mom's two favorite things were talking and reading. They released her from the hospital to a rehab center close to home.

Both my parents were insistent that we should still go to the beach. They argued that if we canceled, we would not get our money back and that my mom would still be in rehab when we returned. They felt I should take Kendall to help me drive and help with costs. Kendall was planning on staying home with my cat and dog. It was a little awkward, but I asked him if he wanted to go with us, and he was allowed to take vacation time.

Kendall and Mackenzie, Hilton Head Island, 2007

So, Kendall slept on the couch in the condo's living room while the girls and I had the bedrooms. It surprised me, but I enjoyed having him with us. The sand on the beach had developed a shelf of sand that you had to step off to get to the water. When we walked on the beach, I did not even have to ask; he stopped and gave me his arm to steady me when I stepped down. When I sat in a chair on the beach, he was there to pull me up. These were things I had depended on my dad to do, but he was not there. Kendall was, and he remembered.

177

When we returned home, Kendall went back to work and back to the basement. He did not mention us getting back together and did not make any physical advances toward me. It was easy to be around him, much easier than when we were married. While we talked one day in the Fall of 2007, I commented that seeing older couples at church saddened me. I told him I had always assumed we would be together forever. Soon after, he mentioned the possibility of remarriage. I told him I would have to pray and think about it. After I prayed, God gave me a list of challenges to give him.

I call them challenges because, before, when given homework by godly counselors, he could never follow through. For me, his follow-through was the biggest challenge. My friends, Dava Lee and John, had been spiritual parents to me, and they had been married almost 45 years. I called and asked them if they would be willing to disciple Kendall. I told Kendall he had to attend Dava Lee's Bible study weekly and do the Bible homework she would give him. She is a retired teacher, so I knew she would hold him to it. He also had to meet with the two of them weekly for discipleship. Lastly, He had to be open about his internet usage. He rose to meet every challenge.

## Kendall

The conditions were completely understandable. I finally realized that I was powerless to change on my own, that simply saying I am sorry was not enough. Repentance means to turn around, to change one's mind on purpose. I needed to be purposeful going forward. So, one of the conditions I happily met was to meet with John and Dava Lee Russell. We met for breakfast and to talk and pray every week. I also got involved with Dava Lee's Bible study. I gladly did the Bible study homework she gave me.

Along with my time alone with God, I was reminded of what grace is all about. They taught me that God loves me and longs to restore His relationship with me regardless of what I had done. As we talked during our weekly breakfasts, I confessed my sins and asked God to heal my heart.

During the Bible Study, Dava Lee had taught about the names of God, one of which is 'Elyashib' - the God who restores. That is what God was doing in me. He was restoring my soul, my heart, and my mind, and soon he would restore my marriage to Penny. God is always faithful, to watch and protect us, to give us His undivided attention when we pray. When we call His name, He will answer. Our lives are meant to be built on the foundation of God and His word. All of our other relationships should resemble our faith in Christ. God's greatest commandments are about relationships. 1 Peter 4:8 says, *"Above all, love each other deeply, because love covers over a multitude of sins."* (NIV) And John 15:12 which says, *"My command is this: Love each other as I have loved you."* (NIV)

A little over a year after moving into the basement, we decided to remarry. When I met John and Dava Lee for weekly counsel and Bible study, I was not trying to check off a box on a to-do list that Penny had given me. Instead, I did it because there are times when your life depends on doing what you need to do to LIVE. Sometimes we have to spend time in a desert to learn how to think, how to live, how to listen, how to hear the voice of God. Sometimes it takes months; sometimes, it takes ten years. Living by the flesh caused my spiritual death and the death of our relationship and marriage. But to God, even death is not final. Resurrection is always possible, whether it be the resurrection of a body or the resurrection of a marriage.

Romans 8:13 *for if you live according to the flesh, you will die; but if by the Spirit you put to death the deeds of the body, you will live.* (NRSV)

# Chapter Twenty-six

**New *(adjective)*: being other than the former or old; made fresh; resumption of a previous act; of dissimilar origin and usually of superior quality** (MW)

Isaiah 43:18-19

*Do not [earnestly] remember the former things; neither consider the things of old. Behold, I am doing a new thing! Now it springs forth; do you not perceive and know it, and will you not give heed to it? I will even make a way in the wilderness and rivers in the desert.* (AMPC)

## Penny

In January 2008, I once again prayed for vision. God gave me the word "New" and scripture to back it up. 2 Corinthians 5:17-18 says, *"Therefore, any person is in Christ, he is a new creation; old things have passed away; behold, all things have become new. Now all things are of God, who has reconciled us to Himself through Jesus Christ..."* (NKJV) And Ezekiel 36:33,36, which says, "Thus says the Lord God, *'On the day that I cleanse you from all your iniquities, I will also enable you to dwell in the cities, and the ruins will be rebuilt... Then the nations which are left all around you shall know that I, the Lord, have rebuilt the ruined places and planted what was desolate. I, the Lord, have spoken it, and I will do it."* (NKJV)

God was rebuilding the ruins. Kendall faithfully attended the Bible Study and completed his homework. He continued to meet with John and Dava Lee weekly as well. Kendall had decided to be transparent, so he gave me all of his passwords, including those to his bank accounts. In addition, he left his computer entirely open to me. I watched character grow in Kendall since 2006, but now Dava Lee and John let me know they felt he was ready.

## Kendall

Do people who are lost know they are lost? I genuinely do not have an answer for that. All I know is that I was lost, and God found me; He restored me. He grabbed me by the shoulders and shook me up a bit. I remember the state of mind I had, the fogginess, and the confusion. I did not like it one bit. Things would not be able to continue the way they were. God would have to change me completely. Looking back, I can honestly say He did. Does that mean I don't have things that are still a struggle? Absolutely not. But I do believe that while I keep my focus on Him, those things do not matter, nor will they be able to remain enshrined in my life. I cannot remember parts of the past. Penny will often ask me about things that happened, and I can't remember them. I also consider that to be a blessing. There are things in our lives we should learn from and not forget. But there are also things best forgotten. I will not sit around and try to remember what I do not remember because of what God is doing NOW and tomorrow.

As the story goes, there was a lost sheep, and the Shepherd left the ninety-nine to find the one.

## Penny

We planned our new wedding day for May 18, 2008. We wanted to have the same date as our first wedding anniversary. It had been seventeen years; twelve years married the first time, and five years apart. David and Ginger came from Georgia to perform the ceremony. No one else was in attendance other than my sister, Mackenzie, Kaitlin, and Linnea.

When we arrived at the gazebo, it was pouring rain. David reminded us that rain was only a blessing from the Lord. Immediately, God reminded me of Joel 2:23, a scripture He had pointed out to me during my journey. It says, *"Be glad then, you children of Zion, and rejoice in the Lord your God; for He has given you the former rain faithfully, and He will cause the rain to come down for you — the former rain and the latter rain in the first month."* (NKJV) The former rain readies the soil for the good seed, and the latter rain ensures a good harvest. God was letting us know we were good ground, and He was planting His seed within us.

We felt communion as a family was essential, and Kendall served each of us in turn. Before the ceremony, Kendall and I had written down all the ways we had hurt each other during our former marriage on paper. During the wedding, we burned the papers signifying, as 1 Corinthians 13:5b says, that love *"keeps no record of wrongs."* (NIV) It is incredible that something we thought of as a symbolic act could be so tangible. In Isaiah 43, He had said, "Do not remember." Forgiveness brings freedom. By burning the "past," we could move forward with the "new," knowing He was doing a new thing in us. And it as held to this day.

Burning the past

184

# Chapter Twenty-seven

**Refined** *(adjective)*: **free from impurities; cultivated** (MW)

Psalm 66:10

*For you, O God, have tested us; You have refined us as silver is refined.* (NKJV)

Penny

I still seek the Lord every new year and throughout the year for His plan for us. I stay in the word. I talk to Him throughout the day. I listen for His voice. I want to be as close as possible. I am by no means perfect. I'm often lazy. I often miss it. But that is okay because, by His grace, I can approach His throne. Lamentations 3:22-23 says, *"Through the Lord's mercies we are not consumed, because His compassions fail not. They are new every morning; great is Your faithfulness."* (NKJV)

Since our wedding in 2008, it has been fourteen years since we remarried. When we remarried, it had been ten years since God spoke to me the promise in 1 Peter 5:10-11, which says, *"But may the God of all grace who called us to His eternal glory by Christ Jesus, after you have a suffered a while, perfect, establish, strengthen and settle you."* (NKJV) He declared the end from the beginning to me through His word. (Is. 46:10 NKJV). He has established, strengthened, and settled us. He is in the process of perfecting us daily. His scriptures have been my source of hope. He gave me His word to help me be brave. The promises in His word changed everything. He did indeed rebuild the ruins as He promised.

In our new marriage, Kendall is my rock -solid and dependable. He has worked hard to support our family financially. Kendall has taken the lead in paying our bills and is open about our finances. Over and over, he has proven himself trustworthy. We are a team and make decisions together. He is honest with us, and he has loved us, never looking back. He continues to lean on God. I have often said in the last fourteen years that it is like living with a different person.

I am also not saying it has been all roses and sunshine for us in the last thirteen years, although there has been plenty of that as well. Our marriage is not perfect. There are plenty of arguments. I am sure the girls can attest to that. The difference is that we ask for forgiveness of each other and from God and keep moving forward. I am also thankful that Kendall is now able to argue. I know that is a strange thing to say, but in the years before our divorce, he would just shut down and shut me out. We have also had some challenging times in the last thirteen years. We have been through several job layoffs in the coal mines, Kendall leaving to find work away from home, new careers, accidents, surgeries, and health issues for both of us. God has never given up on us. He does not change. Hebrews 13:8 says, *"Jesus Christ is the same yesterday, today and forever."* (NKJV) And we have never given up on Him.

You may also wonder about Kendall's diagnosis of bipolar disorder. Was it an accurate diagnosis? At the time, it seemed genuine. Bipolar disorder can be difficult to diagnose. After praying about it, Kendall decided not to go back on medication because it caused fogginess in his thinking and affected his work. However, discontinuing medication is not possible for many people, so always talk with your physician before changing your treatment plan.

There are also several things Kendall has done to maintain his mental health. He exercises and makes sleep a priority. He chooses to work a physically demanding job instead of a stressful management position. He is not medicated but does take a combination of EPA and DHA fish oil, which has proven to help the brain and the heart. He also maintains a varied, well-balanced diet with plenty of fruits and vegetables. He is self-aware and occupies his mind with his creative outlets - writing music and humor. And He stays close to God through prayer and listening to worship music.

God did not promise us a trial-free life. 1 Peter 4:12 says, *Beloved, do not think it strange concerning the fiery trial, which is to try you, as though some strange thing happened to you..."* (NKJV) There will always be trials – with or without God. I would much rather go through them with Him. God has continued to refine Kendall and me in the heat and with pressure. He desires for us to reflect His light and His brilliance to the world. He is always with us in the fire, so we are never alone.

Prayer for God's help in a broken relationship:

Father,
I repent for any wrong I have done toward my spouse. Forgive me for the sin of _____. Reveal any faults in me that I cannot see. I pray the words of my mouth and the meditations of my heart would be acceptable in Your sight, O Lord. (Ps. 19: 14) I pray for my relationship with my spouse, but most importantly, I pray for their relationship with You.

Draw them to Yourself. Help them to hunger and thirst after righteousness and be filled. (Matt. 5:6) May they walk in integrity. Do not let mercy and truth leave them. Bind them around their neck and write them on the tablet of their heart. (Prov. 3:3-4)

Lord, teach us how to put aside pride to avoid strife and arguments. (Prov. 13:10) Give us Your wisdom to repair the breaches and mend our broken relationship. Guard our hearts, but also guard our mouths to avert contention and strife. Give us the strength only You can provide and help us to walk in forgiveness. Amen.

# Epilogue

**Reconciled***(verb)***: to restore to friendship or harmony** (MW)

2 Corinthians 5:18

*Now all things are of God, who has reconciled us to Himself through Jesus Christ and has given us the ministry of reconciliation.* (NKJV)

Penny

Marriage involves two people. Even when one is seeking God, the other may not. When I let go of Kendall in divorce, I let go completely. I wasn't expecting him back. I forgave him and gave Him to God. Yes, we should pray for our spouses, but we still live in a fallen world. Not all marriages are healed and restored (or should be), but that does not mean God does not want to heal and restore you. Even if your marriage ends, it does not mean God has given up on you. He has a specific plan for your life. Jeremiah 29:11 says, *"For surely I know the plans I have for you," says the Lord, "plans for your welfare and not for harm, to give you a future and a hope."* (NRSV) Jesus, by His death on the cross, redeemed us, reconciling us to the Father. Romans 5:8, 10 says, *"But God demonstrates his own love toward us, in that while we were still sinners, Christ died for us. For if, when we were enemies, we were reconciled to God through the death of His Son, much more, having been reconciled, we shall we be saved by His life!"* (NKJV) By His resurrection, He made a way for us to come boldly to the throne of God to obtain mercy and find to help us in our time of need. (Hebrews 4:16 NKJV).

Likewise, not all mental illnesses will play out the same way for everyone, even within the same diagnosis. So, what works for one person may not work for another person. If you or someone you love are having difficulties dealing with life, reach out to your local mental health organization or Christian Counseling Center. In addition, organizations such as Celebrate Recovery or the National Alliance on Mental Health (NAMI) may have groups in your area to offer support as well.

God still heals, but He doesn't always do it in the same way for everyone or in the way you may expect. God healed me from the muscle disease, but I still have calcium deposits hardening within my muscles. God chose to heal my marriage, but He does not heal all marriages. We still live in a sinful world. But God is still good. His grace is still sufficient, and He is still faithful. God met me amid the pain with His grace, kindness, and love. Don't be discouraged. You can trust Him. If you are praying for something, be encouraged; do not give up. Seek Him, and He will always be there.

# Acknowledgements

I want to thank the people who helped us along our journey of faith. Dava Lee and John Russell, Dave and Dr. Ginger Christian, and Drs. Donna and Kevin Renfro were with us through it all. You patiently taught us His word, prayed over us, counseled us, and stood with us. I will be forever grateful.

I have been blessed with an abundance of friends. I do not want to list you all because I am afraid I would leave someone out. These women have also stood with me and prayed for me. They were there in the darkest of times. I am especially grateful to some of these same friends who read first drafts and gave me input and encouragement: Dava Lee Russell, Ginger Christian, Donna Renfro, Cyndi Hobby, Cindy Tvardy, Karen Adkison, Sherry Nakoff, and Theresa Garbe.

Our daughters, Mackenzie and Katie Cochran, were our first readers and have always been supportive and available to help me through editing and computer issues. They are very different, but each is brilliant in their own way and bring diverse perspectives to the table. And to Linnea Adams, my third "daughter," I am so thankful for you. We love each of you more than you can know.

My sister, Cyndi Hobby, has walked this journey with me as well. You have given of yourself and your possessions over and over. I am so thankful to call you my sister and friend.

My parents, Jerry and Yvonne Banner, gave us a home repeatedly during this journey. They cared for my girls when I could not, so I always knew we had a safe place to land. However, I never took that for granted- not everyone has that kind of unconditional love from their parents. Through every difficult time in my life, you both have stood steady, praying over us, and loving us. You are my rocks, and I am so very thankful for your example of a strong, Christian marriage, your strength of character, and your faithfulness to God. Thank you for loving me through it all.

We are also thankful for Kendall's parents, Kendall and Ruth Etta Cochran, for their love, encouragement, prayers and wise counsel. We are thankful for your example of faithfulness and love for God and for each other.

Made in the USA
Columbia, SC
17 May 2025

58064006R00109